# MATH
## *for fun*
# PROJECTS

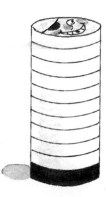

© Aladdin Books Ltd 1999
*Designed and produced by*
Aladdin Books Ltd
28 Percy Street
London W1P 0LD

First published in
the United States
in 1999 by
Copper Beech Books,
an imprint of
The Millbrook Press
2 Old New Milford Road
Brookfield, Connecticut 06804

*Project Editor:* Sally Hewitt
*Editor:* Liz White
*Design:* David West Children's Book Design
*Designer:* Simon Morse
*Photography:* Roger Vlitos
*Illustrator:* Tony Kenyon

Printed in Italy
5 4 3 2 1

ISBN 0-7613-0789-3

# MATH
## *for fun*
# PROJECTS

## Andrew King

## Copper Beech Books
### Brookfield, Connecticut

# CONTENTS

# INTRODUCTION

It's amazing what you can do once you have begun to master math! Have you ever wondered how to write computer games, or plan a journey into space? Would you like to be able to find hidden treasure, find your way through mazes, or plan winning strategies? How could you measure the lines, curves, and shapes that surround you? If you were told that nine-tenths of an iceberg is hidden underwater, could you imagine what that looks like? An understanding of math can reveal how all these things are possible.

Math for Fun Projects introduces you to some of the fascinating feats that math enables you to perform.

You can play Go Fishing to learn about angles, or slice up pizza and learn about fractions. You could use percentages to make a dazzling carpet, or amaze your friends with your x-ray vision using arithmetic.

Through different games and projects you will learn about percentages, symmetry, algebra, setting and sorting, weighing and measuring, and many other mathematical skills. Use the helpful tables at the back of the book to help you if you get stuck.

Follow the STEP-BY-STEP INSTRUCTIONS to help you with the activities.

Use HELPFUL HINTS for tips and clues about the experiments and games.

Look at MORE IDEAS for information about other projects for you to try.

**1** Yellow squares mean this is an easy activity.

**2** Blue squares mean this is a medium activity.

**3** Pink squares mean this is a more difficult activity. You will have to think hard!

# CONTENTS

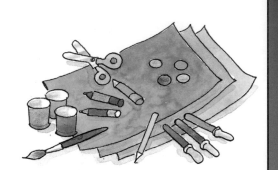

# *Chapter One*

# Exploring Numbers

# NUMBER FACTS

When you were younger, you probably learned different ways of **adding** up two numbers to make 10. Being able to remember number facts quickly, like 6+4=10 and also 2+8=10, can be helpful in solving many **arithmetic** problems.

X-RAY VISION!
If you know your number facts to 7 you will be able to do this trick and pretend that you have x-ray vision! For this trick you will need a die. You could make one.

**1** Cover a cube with colored paper. Stick on shapes for the "number" spots, or you could draw them on.

**2** Throw the die a few times. Each time it comes to rest, make a note of the number that is on the top of the die and the number hidden underneath.

**3** Do you notice a pattern? If you can see a pattern you are ready to do the trick! Say to your audience, "I have x-ray vision and I can see through the die to the hidden number!"

## HELPFUL HINTS

● The secret to this game is that the opposite sides of the die always add up to **equal** 7. If you see a 3 at the top of the die then the hidden face must be 4 because...

$$3+4=7$$

It is a bit like trying to solve a problem like this: $3+?=7$.

MORE IDEAS

● This is like the x-ray vision trick. It uses the same pattern. Can you work it out? You need two dice. Place one on top of the other. The top face and the hidden faces in the middle and underneath will add up to... you've got it — 14! That's because $7+7=14$. You can say, "I know what all three hidden numbers add up to!"

● What is it here? If you can solve the sum $3+?=14$, you can find out.

# SUMMING UP

We often use the word sum to describe any arithmetic problem. The sum is the total of a list of numbers that have been added together.

FIFTEEN!

Fifteen is quite a tricky game. You need to be good at adding up single digit numbers in your head. Make a game board like this with colored cardboard and you are ready to start.

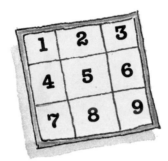

**1** To make two sets of pieces, cut out five circles of colored cardboard and five more of a different color.

**2** Cut a line from the edge to the center of each circle. Slide one cut edge behind the other and stick it in place to make a cone.

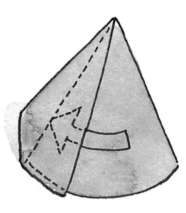

← Cut along the dashed line

**3** Each player chooses a set of pieces and takes turns to cover one square at a time. The winner of the game is the first person to make a total of 15. If you go over 15, you are "bust" and lose.

# HELPFUL HINTS

● If you choose one of the larger numbers to start with, be careful, it is easy to go bust!

● Try and make 15 yourself, but remember, your opponent is also trying to make 15. Can you stop them at the same time?

## MORE IDEAS

● Is it better to go first or second in this game? Can you figure out a way to make sure that you win every time?

## TWENTY-ONE OR BUST!

● This is another exciting game a little bit like Fifteen. You will need a deck of cards. (The ace counts as 1 or 11. The face cards – Jacks, Queens, and Kings – are worth 10.) Draw two cards from the deck. You can then decide to take another card, or "stay." The object of the game is to get as close to 21 as possible without going over.

# COUNTING DOWN

Can you count backward? That's easy! Can you count backward in 2s... from any number? Start on 20. Try 105. What about 1,005? Now try counting backward in 3s! Counting backward is one way of **subtracting,** or taking away.

THE BLACK SPOT!

Some people say that this is an ancient pirate game. You will need to do a lot of backward counting to make sure that you don't lose and walk the plank! Play this with a friend.

**1** Find ten white checkers and one black checker for the black spot. Draw pirate faces onto circles of cardboard and stick a face onto each white checker. Stack all the pieces in a column with the black spot at the bottom.

**2** Decide who is going first. Each player takes turns to remove either one, two, or three pieces. The object of the game is to make your opponent pick the black spot, so they have to walk the plank!

14

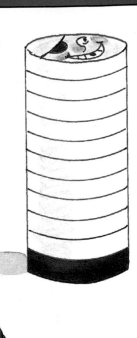

# HELPFUL HINTS

● One way of getting better at this game is to search for winning patterns. If you were the winner, try to remember how you started. What did your opponent do next?

## MORE IDEAS

● Is it better to go first or second in this game? How would the way you play the game change if another piece was added to the stack? How would the way you play the game change if you could only remove one or two pieces each turn?

## SWEET SIXTEEN

● Another great game like The Black Spot is Sweet Sixteen. It can be played with a calculator. Start with 16 on the display and take turns to subtract 1, 2, or 3. If you manage to leave your opponent with 1 on the display then you have won the game.

# VALUE YOUR DIGITS!

Numbers are made up of digits like words are made up of letters. But where a digit is placed in a number affects its value. A two digit number is made up of tens and ones. The 2 in 25 has a value of 20 (two tens), the 5 has a value of 5 (five ones).

## DRAW A NUMBER

**1** You can design your own numbers to show the value of the digits. You will need some graph paper and some pens, pencils, paint... or whatever you like to help with your design.

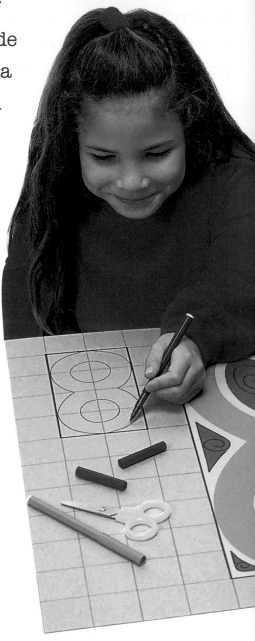

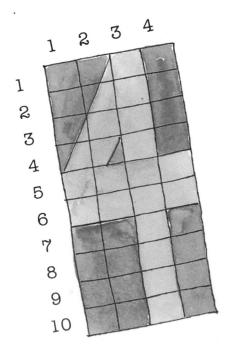

**2** Choose a two digit number — what about 46? Draw a rectangle of 40 small squares for the 4 digit and a rectangle of 6 small squares for the 6. Design each digit inside its rectangle.

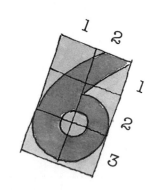

**3** Decorate your digits with interesting colors and patterns. Now you can see the value of each digit in your two digit number at a glance.

5

8

# HELPFUL HINTS

● For a number like 40 there are many rectangles that you could draw. You could choose a rectangle with two sides of 4 and two sides of 10, because 4x10=40 squares. You can draw any rectangle where the side lengths can be multiplied to make 40 squares. Sides of 5 and 8 are also possible because 5x8=40 squares.

## MORE IDEAS

● Find some more paper with very small squares. Instead of just having a rectangular area for your digit, cut out the correct number of squares in any shape and design your digit inside the shape.

● You could color in the number of squares you need to make your digit. So for the 3 of 30 color in 30 squares.

# PLACE YOUR DIGITS

Numbers can have any amount of digits! 841 is a three digit number. The first digit shows how many hundreds there are. The 8 has the value of eight hundred. If you rearrange the digits like this — 481 — the 8 has the value of eighty. What value does the 8 have in the number 418?

THREE CARD TRICK
You can play this game with one or two friends.

**1** Using colored cardboard make a score card like the one on this page. Now make a set of cards, draw on the digits 1 to 9. Everyone takes three cards.

**2** Rearrange your cards. What is the largest number you can make? The player who has the largest number scores a point.

**3** What is the smallest number you can make? The player with the smallest number scores a point.

**4** On the scorecard write down as many different numbers as you can make with your three cards. Score a point for each number.

**5** Place the numbers in order from the smallest to the largest. Score an extra bonus point for doing this correctly. Could this player have scored more points?

## 3 CARD TRICK

| Digit | 5 | 2 | 6 | points |
|---|---|---|---|---|
| Largest Number | 652 | | | 1 |
| Smallest Number | 256 | | | 1 |
| Different Numbers | 625 | | | 1 |
| | 562 | | | 1 |
| | 256 | | | 1 |
| | 652 | | | 1 |
| Smallest to Largest | 256 | | | |
| | 562 | | | |
| | 625 | | | 1 |
| | 652 | | | |
| Total Points | | | | 7 |

## HELPFUL HINTS

● When comparing numbers with the same amount of digits to find which is larger, look at the digits on the left side of the number first. The larger the digit the larger the number. If the digit is the same then compare the next one. Repeat this until you find the larger number.

# 5 4 6 8

Thousands — 5

Hundreds — 4 (Tens)

Tens — 6

Ones — 8

MORE IDEAS
● The 5 in 5,468 has a value of five thousand. How many different numbers can you make with these four digits?

# BIG, BIGGER, BIGGEST

Mathematicians use signs to show when a number is smaller or bigger than another number. They are called **inequality signs** and they look like this < or like this >. Whatever is on the open side is larger. For example 10>5.

HI SCORE!

You can play Hi Score on your own or with lots of friends. The object of the game is to make the number on the right of the scorecard as large as you can. This three digit number is your Hi Score.

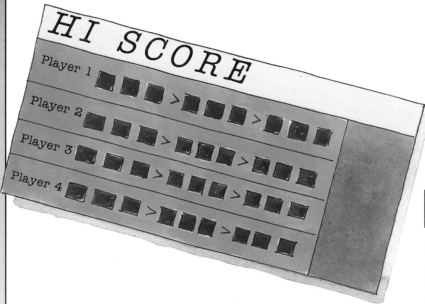

**1** Copy this Hi Score game board. You could make it with colored cardboard and magic marker. Put your name and your friends' names in as the players.

**2** Take turns to throw a die. Think carefully about where to place the digit you have thrown. You can't change it later.

**3** Each line on the scorecard is a mathematical sentence. You only score if the sentence is true! If your digits were like this 621>451>233 you would score 233. If the numbers were not in the correct order like this 631>423>551 you would score nothing!

## HELPFUL HINTS

● The most important digit is the one you put in the hundreds place. If you roll a 6 where would be the best place to put it?

● The number on the open side of the inequality sign, is always the larger one.

**BIGGER > smaller**

MORE IDEAS
● Invent a game called Lo Score. What will your board look like? Can you write out the rules to go with it? What number would be best to put in the hundreds place of the first column?

# SIGN OF THE TIMES

**Multiplying** numbers is a quick way of adding the same number many times.

That's why some people say "times" to mean multiplication. The multiplication sign looks like this x. If we want to figure out what six 2s are, we don't need to write 2+2+2+2+2+2. We can write 6x2 instead.

MOUNTAIN MULTIPLICATION
Climb the mountain to find the number at the peak.

**1** Cut out a triangle of cardboard and draw four "rocks" along the bottom, three rocks in the next row and two rocks in the third row. Cut out some "snow" and stick it on the peak.

**3** Add poster putty to the back of each circle and stick the first four onto the bottom row. To find the next number up the mountain, multiply the two numbers below it.

**2** Stick two triangles on the back for support and make trees for the sides. Cut out ten small circles of paper and write the numbers 2, 1, 2, 3 on the first four circles.

# HELPFUL HINTS

● To find the number that is missing underneath the 12 (left), it is helpful to think about it as a multiplication problem like this...

**2 x ? = 12**

**4** The number above the 2 and 1 will be 2 because 2x1=2. Figure out what all three numbers are on the next row.

**5** Write them on the circles and stick them on. Keep repeating this, until you reach the top.

## MORE IDEAS

● Can you figure out all the numbers that cover the mountain (above left) if you only have some of the numbers half way up the slope?

● Make your own mountain problem and get your friends to reach the top.

● Put 13 at the peak. Fill in the numbers on the mountain. What do you notice?

## BUILD A PYRAMID

● Put some small numbers on four blocks. These are the base of your pyramid. Multiply the numbers as you did on the mountain and stick the answers on the next layer of blocks. Find the number at the top of the pyramid.

# DO THE OPPOSITE

Have your parents ever said that you always do the opposite of what they tell you? When this happens in mathematics, it is called the inverse. The inverse of adding 3 is taking away 3. Do you know the inverse of multiplying by 2? Yes! **Dividing** by 2. What is the inverse of dividing by 4?

WHAT'S THAT NUMBER?

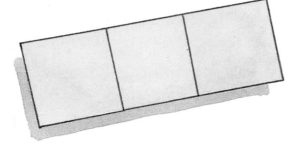

**1** Cut some cardboard into small strips about as big as the one in the picture. Fold each strip to make three sections. Shade in the middle section lightly with a colored pencil.

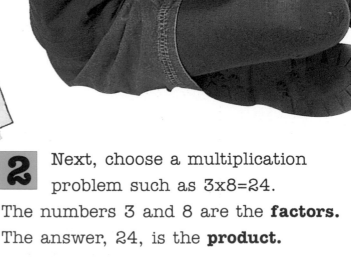

**2** Next, choose a multiplication problem such as 3x8=24. The numbers 3 and 8 are the **factors.** The answer, 24, is the **product.**

**3** Write the product in the middle square and the factors on either side. Make a pile of about 20 cards like this with different multiplication problems on each.

**4** The first player picks up a card and folds one of the factors behind. The second player tries to figure out what the hidden number is. If they are correct, they win the card. Keep going until one player has all the cards.

60 180 3

**MORE IDEAS**
● You could play the same game with more difficult numbers.

**HANDS DOWN**
● This is another good game that you can play using factors and products. Instead of folding over a factor, cover one of the numbers with your hand. You could cover either the product or one of the factors on each side. Can your friends guess what number is hidden?

# HARD TIMES!

Being able to remember multiplication facts quickly is very useful when trying to solve number problems. You can try to memorize the tables from the chart at the back of the book. But, here are some games that make learning your times tables much more fun!

## CARD TRICKS

This is a game for two or more players. You will need a deck of cards with all the face cards removed.

**1** Place the cards face down on the table. Choose a multiplication table, for example, the four times table.

**2** Now, take turns to look at two cards. Is the product of the two numbers on the cards in the four times table?

**3** If it is, keep the pair and take another turn. If not, turn the cards back over, it's the next player's turn. The winner is the player with the most pairs.

**4** You could keep the cards 2 and 6 and have another turn. Could you keep the 3 and 7?

# CHICKEN RACE
The object of this game is to make the biggest score you can.

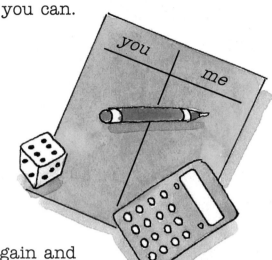

**1** You will need a die, a calculator, and a pencil and paper to draw out the chart. The first player throws the die and makes a note of the number.

**2** Throw the die again and multiply the two numbers together. Keep throwing the die, multiplying the number on the die with your total. You must decide when to stop because... if a 1 is thrown, you get 0 for that turn! Use a calculator to check that your multiplication is correct.

**Dare you keep throwing the die... or are you chicken?!**

SCORING
CHICKEN RACE
You could note your
scores like this —

| 3 | |
|---|---|
| | x4 |
| 12 | |
| | x2 |
| 24 | |
| | x5 |
| 120 | stay! |

But things
could
go wrong...

| 4 | |
|---|---|
| | x2 |
| 8 | |
| | x1 | no score! |

# BIG TIME OPERATOR

If you have tried the other activities in this book, you will know more about addition, subtraction, multiplication, division, inverses, sums, factors, and products than when you started! Are you skillful enough to use what you know to solve some of these number explosion problems?

## NUMBER EXPLOSIONS

**1** How many ways can you make 10? You have probably already thought of quite a few ways of making 10 by adding a couple of single digit numbers. But can you think of more interesting ways of making 10?

$2 \times 4 + 2 \longrightarrow$

$1 + 8 + 1 \longrightarrow$

**10**

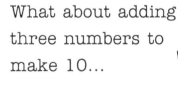

What about adding three numbers to make 10...

**2** Use bright colored cardboard to design a huge explosion like the one in the picture and put 10 or any number you choose in the middle.

How about adding a number then subtracting another?

← 1 + 12 - 3

Try starting from 1,000. Can you add, divide, subtract then multiply a number to make 10?

## HELPFUL HINTS

● It is easy to be a big time operator and use all the operations if you remember some simple facts about the operations:

**addition is the inverse of subtraction**
**multiplication is the inverse of division**

● What happens when you add or subtract 0?
● What happens when you divide or multiply by 1?
● What happens if you multiply or divide by 0?

### FURTHER IDEAS
● How can you use the numbers 1, 2, 3, and 4 once each to make 10? One easy way is to add them all together 1+2+3+4=10.
● Use different operations and find other ways to make 10.

1+2+3+4 → 10

# GAMES GALORE!

How many board games do you know? Which is your favorite? For some of the games in the book you need to use addition, subtraction, multiplication, and division. Some games use dice, spinners, cards, and pieces. Can you invent your own game?

DESIGN YOUR OWN GAME

**1** You might need pencils, pens, cardboard, something to make the pieces with — it all depends on the game you want to make. How creative can you be?

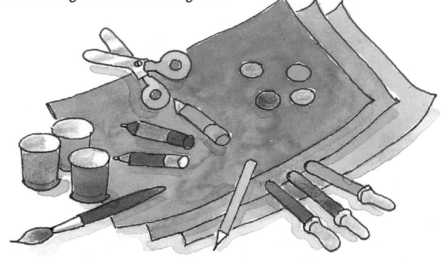

**2** You might want to make a counting game. The game might need some cards that give the players different directions like "Go to Jail!" or "Start Again."

**3** Decide who the game is going to be for: yourself, some adults, a friend, or a little brother or sister... don't make it too hard if it's for your little brother or sister!

**4** Now give your game a theme — it could be animals or sports — what about space?

**5** Now write down the rules. What do you have to do to win? Can you think of an exciting name?

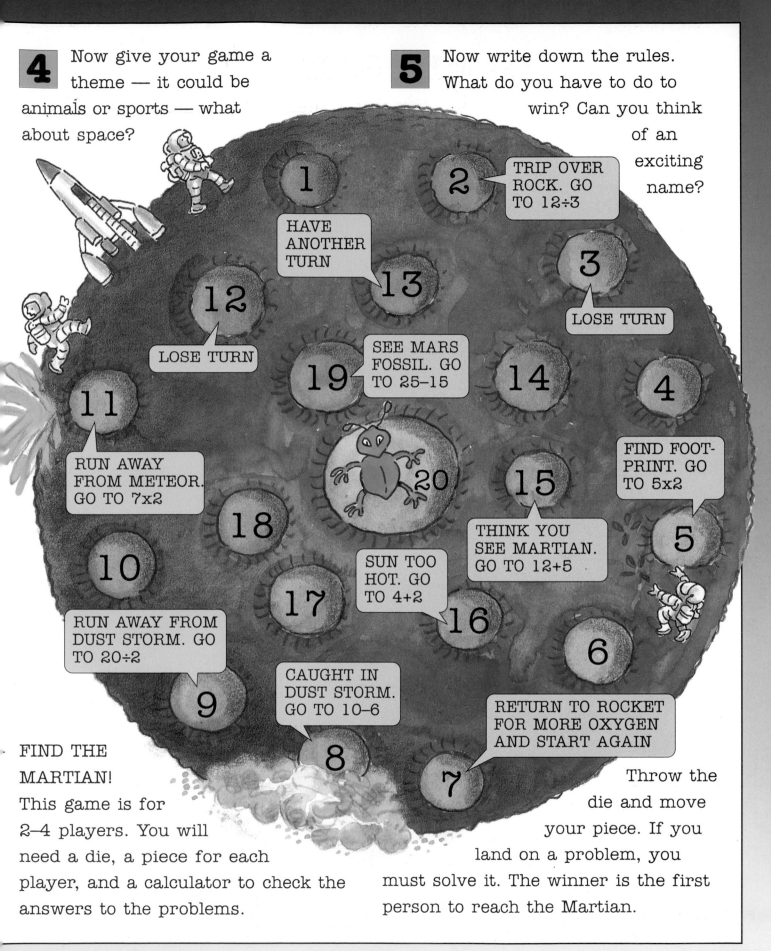

1

2 — TRIP OVER ROCK. GO TO 12÷3

3 — LOSE TURN

HAVE ANOTHER TURN

13

12 — LOSE TURN

19 — SEE MARS FOSSIL. GO TO 25−15

14

4

11 — RUN AWAY FROM METEOR. GO TO 7x2

20

15 — THINK YOU SEE MARTIAN. GO TO 12+5

FIND FOOT-PRINT. GO TO 5x2

5

18

10

17 — SUN TOO HOT. GO TO 4+2

16

RUN AWAY FROM DUST STORM. GO TO 20÷2

9 — CAUGHT IN DUST STORM. GO TO 10−6

8

7 — RETURN TO ROCKET FOR MORE OXYGEN AND START AGAIN

6

FIND THE MARTIAN!
This game is for 2–4 players. You will need a die, a piece for each player, and a calculator to check the answers to the problems.

Throw the die and move your piece. If you land on a problem, you must solve it. The winner is the first person to reach the Martian.

# PROBLEMS, PROBLEMS...

When you have a problem to solve, like finding out how many hairs you have on your head, the best way to tackle it is to make a careful guess, or an estimate, of the answer. Then, while you are tackling the problem, keep a note of any calculations you make. This will help you to check back if you make a mistake.

A NOVEL IDEA

**1** Try to work out how many pages there are in a very thick book without looking at the page numbers! Make an estimate. What do you think... 100, 325, 809?

**3** You can look at the page numbers to check your answer. Can you think of a better way of solving the problem?

**2** You could count the number of pages in one chapter. Next find the number of chapters. Now multiply the number of pages in a chapter by the number of chapters. This will give you an answer.

## PARTY ANIMALS

**1** If you have a party for your friends you will need to make some calculations. How many friends will be coming? Will you go to the zoo?

**2** What will it cost? How much allowance do you have? Is it enough? What do you need to buy? Do you need a loan from your parents?

**3** Keep a careful note of the costs and how much you have spent.

| | |
|---|---|
| Price of zoo ticket | $7.50 |
| Number of friends | 4 |
| Total cost of tickets | $_____ |
| Allowance | $15.00 |
| Need loan of | $_____ |

## GO FOR BROKE

Imagine you have just won a million dollars — but you have to spend it within one week! What would you spend it on?

**1** Find some catalogs and magazines and decide how you are going to spend the money.

**2** You need to prove that you have spent all the money in one week. How are you going to show that you have spent all that money?

RECEIPT

SPORTS CAR

$30,000

# CONTENTS

# Chapter Two

# Making Fractions

# WHAT IS A FRACTION?

A **fraction** is a part of a whole thing like a cake, an apple, or a school class. If a cake has had a slice cut out of it, it is not whole. The slice is a part, or a fraction, of the whole cake. If an apple is cut up, it

is not a whole. The pieces are fractions of the whole.

## APPLE GETS THE CHOP

**1** This apple has been cut into two equal pieces. It has been cut in **half**. A half is a fraction and we write it like this $1/2$.

**2** This apple has been cut into four equal pieces. It has been cut into quarters. A quarter is a fraction too. We write it like this $1/4$.

# PIZZA SLICES

**1** Trace around a plate on construction paper to make two circles. Decorate both circles like a pizza and cut them out.

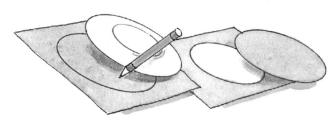

**2** Fold one pizza exactly in half. Cut along the fold to make two halves.

**3** Repeat step 2 for the second pizza. Now fold each half exactly in half and cut along the folds to make four quarters.

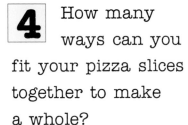

**4** How many ways can you fit your pizza slices together to make a whole?

## MORE IDEAS

● Try to put three quarters and one half together. You will get one pizza with a quarter left over. You can write this as 1 1/4 or as a fraction 5/4. Fractions bigger than a whole are called **improper fractions.**

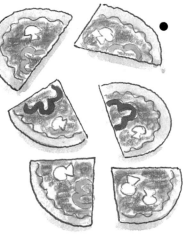

# ADDING FRACTIONS

Fractions can be added like any other number. To make a whole pizza (see page 37,) you needed to add the fractions of the pizza together. There are many different ways of adding fractions together to make a whole.

## BUILD A FRACTION WALL

**1** These children are building a fraction wall using blocks of different sizes.

You can make a small fraction wall from colored cardboard.

**2** Copy these shapes onto the cardboard and cut them all out. You need one whole block, two 1/2 blocks, three 1/3 blocks, four 1/4 blocks, five 1/5 blocks, and six 1/6 blocks.

1/6

1/5

1/4

1/3

1/2

1

**Remember that each layer of the wall must be exactly equal to a whole block.**

**3** You can use these blocks to build your own wall. Start with the whole block on the bottom and build your wall using a mixture of fractions.

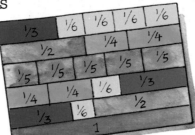

# HELPFUL HINTS

● Match all the layers against the whole block. If they fit exactly the sum is correct.

## MORE IDEAS

● When the wall is as high as possible, write down the fraction names of the blocks you have used on each layer.

● Extend your wall by making other fraction blocks. How about a ninth — $1/9$?

# FAIR SHARES

A fraction can also be part of a group of things. Have you ever been asked to share some candy with your brother or sister? When you have divided the candy equally with another person you have divided the candy in half. A half is a fraction of the whole group of candy.

GRAB!

This is a fun fraction game for two, three, or four players. You will need about 50 small pieces or you could use dried beans.

**1** Put the pieces in a container. The first player grabs a handful of beans.

**2** Try to divide the handful into two equal groups or halves. If you can, you score two points.

= **2 points.**

**3** Can you divide the beans into four equal groups, or quarters? If you can, score four more points.

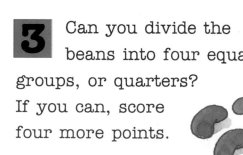

= **4 points.**

**4** If you can complete steps 1, 2, and 3 you can go on to the bonus round! If you can divide your beans into three equal groups, or thirds, score a bonus of three points.

**= 3 points.**

**5** When you have taken a turn, put the beans back and the next player takes a turn.

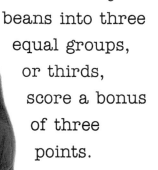

## MORE IDEAS

● Is 17 a good number to grab? What about 16? What about 12? Which would earn you the highest score?

● Keep playing the game. Note down the numbers that score the most points. Can you discover the numbers that are best for sharing into equal groups?

# DECIMAL FRACTIONS

**Decimals** are another way of writing fractions. You have probably seen a lot of decimal numbers before without realizing! If you have watched any sporting events on television, the distances jumped or thrown are usually shown as a decimal number.

**9.83**

A decimal number is one with a **decimal point.** The point separates the whole numbers on the left from the numbers less than 1 on the right.

**1** There are ten tenths between 0 and 1. The object of this game is to point to the correct place on the number line.

POINT IT OUT
Try this guessing game with your friends.

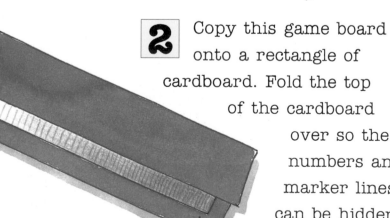

**2** Copy this game board onto a rectangle of cardboard. Fold the top of the cardboard over so the numbers and marker lines can be hidden.

**3** The first player covers the side showing the tenths and asks the second player to find a decimal from 0.1 to 0.9. It could be 0.4 for example. The second player has to estimate where it might be on the number line.

**4** Uncover the line and see if they managed to point it out!

MORE IDEAS

● If you have a calculator, find out what happens if you try to show a half on the display.

The buttons you need to press to do this are 1÷2=. You will see 0.5 on the display.

Do the same with a quarter, 1÷4=.
You will see 0.25.

Try other fractions and see what happens.

● What happens if you try 1÷5? What fraction is this?

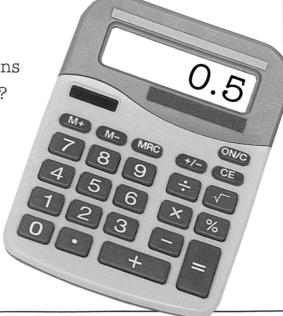

# LARGER OR SMALLER?

How do you decide if one decimal number is larger than another? With whole numbers like 134 and 273 you can compare the size of the digits starting on the left. 273 is bigger than 134 because the 2 digit is worth more than the 1 digit. You can compare decimal numbers like 23.75 and 14.28 in the same way.

## DIABOLICAL DECIMALS

**1** The object of this game is to make the largest number. If you win draw a happy face. First draw a chart like this one. The first player throws the die and decides where to place the digit.

 = You win

😦 = You lose

**2** Remember to put a big digit on the left. Where would you put a 5? Be careful, you might throw a 6 next turn!

**3** The second player throws and also decides where to place their digit. This continues until the four digit number is completed.

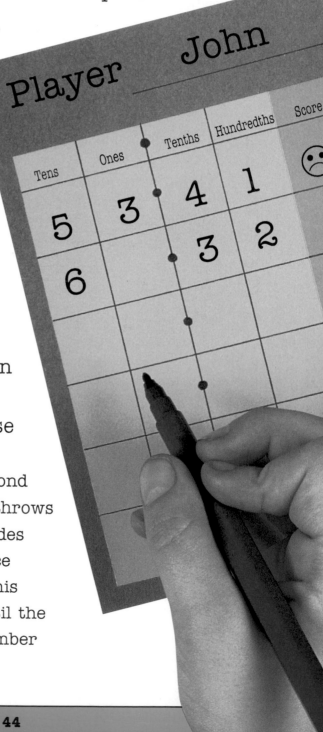

Player _____ John

| Tens | Ones | Tenths | Hundredths | Score |
|------|------|--------|------------|-------|
| 5 | 3 | 4 | 1 | 😦 |
| 6 | | 3 | 2 | |
| | | | | |
| | | | | |
| | | | | |
| | | | | |

It's Emma's turn to throw. Who do you think will win this game?

# HELPFUL HINTS

- To find out who has won compare the digits on the left. If they are the same move to the next digits to their right. If they still match repeat the process until you have found out who has made the larger number.

## MORE IDEAS

- There are some interesting variations to Diabolical decimals that you can play.
- The winner could be the player who makes the smallest number.
- You can also play a game in teams of two. Take turns to throw the die and try to get your numbers as close together as possible. The winning team is the one with the smallest difference between their pairs of numbers. Use a calculator to check.

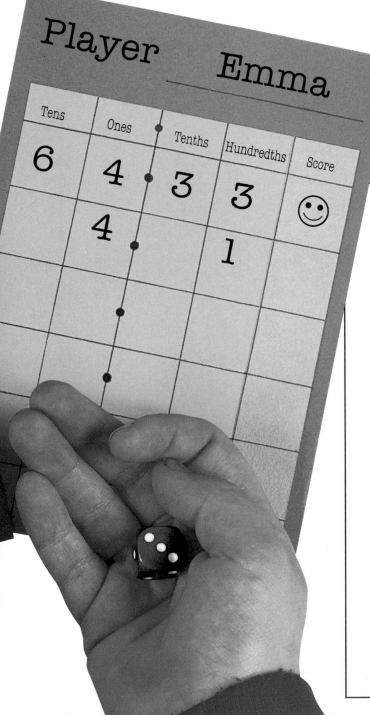

Player _____ Emma

| Tens | Ones | Tenths | Hundredths | Score |
|------|------|--------|------------|-------|
| 6 | 4 | 3 | 3 | ☺ |
|  | 4 |  | 1 |  |
|  |  |  |  |  |
|  |  |  |  |  |
|  |  |  |  |  |
|  |  |  |  |  |

Team 1

| 4 | 3 | 6 | 2 | ☺ |
| 4 | 2 | 5 | 1 |  |

Team 2

| 6 | 2 | 6 | 5 |  |
| 6 | 5 | 6 | 3 | ☹ |

# ADDING DECIMALS

Adding decimal numbers is as easy as adding whole numbers. The key to making it easy is remembering to add digits from the same position in the number system. In other words, adding tens to tens, ones to ones, tenths to tenths, and hundredths to hundredths.

> **If the answer to 23 + 34 = 57 then 2.3 + 3.4 = 5.7**

SPLOTCH IT!
This game is all about adding up tenths. Tenths are shown by the first digit to the right of the decimal point. Remember, ten tenths make 1.

**1** Make a set of splotch cards. Cut out a stack of 20 splotches from some colored cardboard.

**2** Write in the numbers. Make sure the numbers on the edges of the splotch all add up to the total in the center.

**3** Take turns to hold up a splotch card with one of the corners covered.

## HELPFUL HINTS
● To make sure you are putting the correct totals in the center of your cards it might be a good idea to use a calculator to check the answer. Remember to press the decimal point!

**4** Can your opponent work out what the hidden number is? You could solve it like this 0.5 + 0.4 + ? = 1

## MORE IDEAS
● You could change this game around by covering the total in the middle. Are you still as good?

● See if you can figure out what is in the middle of this card. You could try to solve it like this 0.6+0.3+1.1=?.

1·1

0·6

0·3

# PERCENTAGES

**Percentages** are a way of showing fractions as a part of one hundred. A half of a hundred is fifty. We call fifty out of a hundred, fifty percent. The symbol mathematicians use for percent looks like this %. Twenty-five is a quarter of a hundred, so a quarter can be written as 25%. A **tenth** of a hundred is 10. How do you think a tenth would be written as a percentage?

## PERCENTAGE PATTERNS

Take a look at this hundred

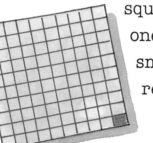

square. Each one of the small squares represents 1%.

**1** If half of the hundred square is filled in, 50 squares will be covered, or 50%.

**2** We could show 50% like this, but there are many fun ways to show it on a hundred square!

**3** Find some graph paper and see if you can design an unusual pattern that covers exactly 50% of the hundred square.

## HELPFUL HINTS
● For 50% of the hundred square to be covered you must color 50 small squares. When you plan your design mark the squares lightly with a pencil. It is easier to make a change if you have miscounted!

MORE IDEAS
● Try some different percentage amounts to cover your hundred square. What about a design that shows 30% of the square? How about 51%?
● Make your design as interesting as you can.

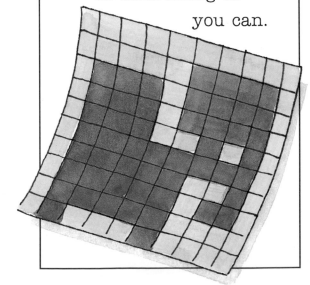

# ESTIMATING PERCENTAGES

Making an **estimate** is like making a careful guess. People make estimates using percentages.

If a teacher says "about fifty percent of the class have done their homework" she estimates that about half the class have done it!

$$\frac{\text{Amount}}{\text{Whole}} \times 100 = \text{Percentage}$$

HOW SQUARE ARE YOUR EYES?
This hundred square represents the whole day, 24 hours. You can make your own one to find out how you spend your time.

**At School**

**Sleeping**

**Eating**

**1** You will need a plain piece of square paper and some coloring pens to fill in your own grid.
First, fold the paper in half and keep folding in strips. Unfold the paper and fold in the other direction. Open out the paper and you will find that you have made squares. Mark out a big square of 10x10 small squares to make a hundred square grid.

**2** Estimate the percentage of time you think you spend watching T.V. Shade in your estimate on the grid. For example, if you think it is 5%, color in five squares on the grid.

**3** Next, estimate the percentage of the day spent doing other things like eating, sleeping, playing, and working. Shade in the amounts on your hundred square.

Watching T.V.

Playing

Make a list of your estimates like this before you color your grid.

| | |
|---|---|
| Sleeping | 45% |
| Eating | 7% |
| Playing | 15% |
| School | 23% |
| T.V. | 10% |

## HELPFUL HINTS

● Make sure your whole hundred square gets covered. There shouldn't be any gaps — you are always doing something, even if it is sleeping!

● Use a different bright color for each activity.

**4** Compare your finished hundred square with the one in this picture. Have you estimated that you are sleepier or more wide awake?!

MORE IDEAS

● How good is your estimate?

● Find an older friend or an adult who is really good at math. Ask them to calculate the real percentages of how you spend your day!

● How does your estimate compare?

# MAKING 100%

Have you ever heard of anything being described as 100% pure or 100% genuine? 100% means everything, the whole. The whole doesn't have to be made up of 100 separate pieces. Do you remember that 50% is another way of describing a half? 50% of 80 is 40. 50% of 36 is 18. What is 50% of 90?

MAGIC CARPETS
Some traditional carpet designs from around the world use many colors and patterns.

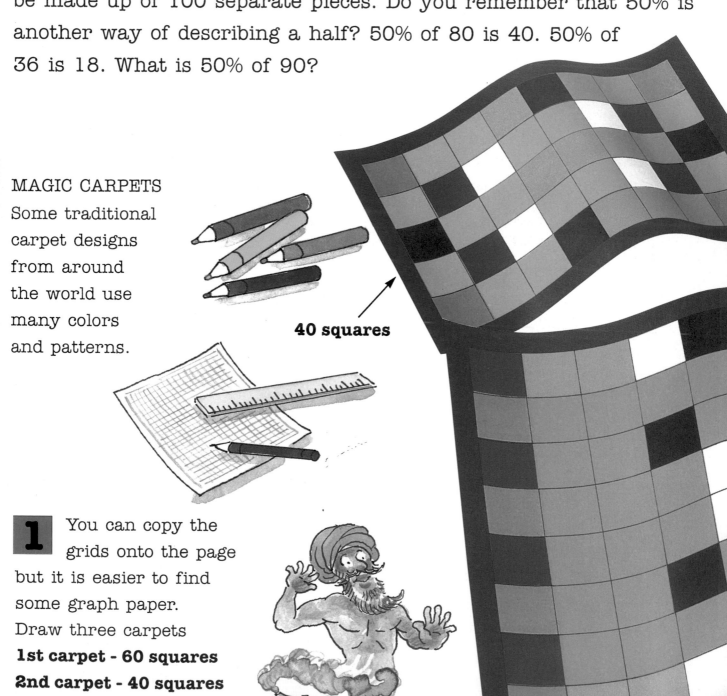

**40 squares**

**1** You can copy the grids onto the page but it is easier to find some graph paper. Draw three carpets

**1st carpet - 60 squares**
**2nd carpet - 40 squares**
**3rd carpet - 80 squares**

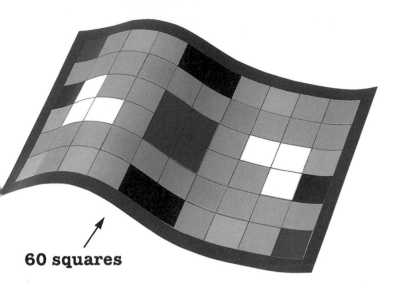

**60 squares**

**2** Design your own carpet pattern using six colors. Your design must be 50% blue, 10% red, 10% yellow, 10% green, 10% black, 10% white. Check the percentages that have been used for the carpets in this picture.

# HELPFUL HINTS

● If you are stuck, find out what 50% of your carpet is.

● For the first carpet of 60 squares, 50% is half the total — which is 30 squares!

● To find 10% divide the total, 60 by 10. This gives the answer 6. So, 30 squares will be blue, 6 red, 6 yellow, 6 green, 6 black, and 6 white.

**80 squares**

MORE IDEAS

● Design some more carpets. This time make them more intricate by dividing some squares in half.

# RATIOS

**Ratios** can be used to show the amounts in which different things are combined to make a whole. Paints are very often made up of mixtures of the primary colors — red, blue, and yellow. To get an exact shade they are mixed according to a particular ratio. Two parts red to one part blue makes purple. The parts can be measured with teaspoons. You would write it like this 2:1 red blue.

## MIXING IT

**1** You can make your own color chart by some careful mixing. Choose two colors.

**2** Make a chart showing where you will paint your different tints. Show the ratio of different paints you will use.

**Red : Yellow**

Red

3:2

1:1

2:7

1:8

Yellow

**3** If you are mixing paints in the ratio of 3:2 use a small spoon to measure out three parts red to two parts yellow and mix carefully.

**4** Paint a small sample of the different mixtures into each area to complete your reference chart.

# HELPFUL HINTS

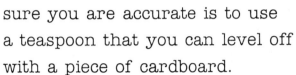

● When you are mixing the colors make sure the amount you use for each part is always the same! The easiest way to make sure you are accurate is to use a teaspoon that you can level off with a piece of cardboard.

● When you have used one mixture make sure you wash your brush carefully, otherwise you will finish up with muddy looking colors that all look the same!

## MORE IDEAS
● Find different ways of mixing the three primary colors together.

● What does 1 red : 4 yellow : 1 blue look like?

● Which is your favorite color? What is the ratio of the three colors?

● Try to work out the ratios of the color of your favorite crayon. Use different ratios until you can find a match.

# MORE MIXING

Ratios can also show how more than two quantities can be mixed. You probably use ratios a lot without realizing it. If you wanted to record how flour, butter, and sugar were combined to make some cookies it could be written like this 3:2:2 three parts flour, two parts butter, and two parts sugar. The parts could be measured with cups or spoons. You could do the same for mixing drinks.

**SHAKEN NOT STIRRED**
You can make some fantastic fruit drinks by mixing ingredients carefully!

**1** Try starting with orange juice, apple juice, and seltzer. A delicious combination is five parts apple, two parts orange, and three parts seltzer. You can make the drink like this.

**2** First find a small container, like an eggcup, and a large glass. Fill the eggcup, or the measurer you have chosen, five times with apple juice and tip it into the glass.

**3** Now add two eggcups of the orange juice.

| Apple | Orange | Seltzer | Good/Bad? |
|-------|--------|---------|-----------|
| 5 | 2 | 3 | Excellent |
| | | | |
| | | | |

## HELPFUL HINTS

● Remember to keep a careful note of the number of parts you have mixed together and the mixtures you liked. You might want to note this in a table.

**4** Last of all pour in three eggcups of seltzer. Stir it and taste. Mmmmm....

**5** What do you think? Now try your own mixture.

### MORE IDEAS

● What about trying other ingredients to make that perfect drink? You could try some other fruit juices, lemonade can be nice, or what about a little vinegar!

● Make sure you ask an adult if you want to try these or any other ingredients in your drink.

# PERFECTLY PROPORTIONED

Many things in nature, including people, grow in a very precise way. For example, the size of everyone's head has a particular relationship, or proportion, to their height. If you measure around your head and multiply that length by three, the answer you get will be roughly the same as your height.

ARE YOU SIX FEET TALL?
You may not believe it but you are about six feet tall! In fact, nearly everyone is! Using ratios you can prove that most people are about six feet tall.

**1** Find a long strip of cardboard or paper and ask an adult to stand next to it. Have the adult take off a shoe. Place the heel of the shoe on the floor, toe pointing upward against the cardboard.

**2** Mark where the end of the toe is with a pen then move the shoe up so that the heel is where your mark is.

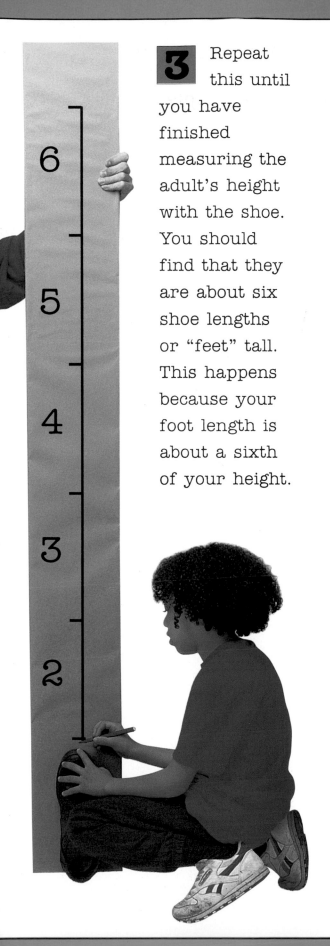

**3** Repeat this until you have finished measuring the adult's height with the shoe. You should find that they are about six shoe lengths or "feet" tall. This happens because your foot length is about a sixth of your height.

## HELPFUL HINTS

● The proportions of younger growing bodies are not usually the same as an adult's. You can try this with your friends but it might be more reliable to test it on an adult.

### MORE IDEAS

● Another fascinating body ratio is sometimes known as Pythagoras's navel. This ratio compares a person's height with the height of the navel from the ground.

● It is usually in the ratio of 1:1.6

● This is a very special ratio called the Golden Mean. It is often found in nature and was considered by the ancient Greeks to have divine properties.

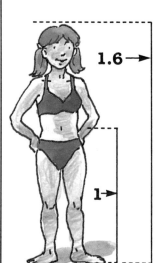

● Measure your height, then the height of your navel from the floor. Divide the first height by the second. How close to 1.6 is the result? Is your body of divine proportion?

# CONTENTS

# *Chapter Three*

# Discovering Patterns

# NUMBER PATTERNS

You can find patterns everywhere in numbers. Even numbers can be divided in two without leaving any remainder. Squared numbers are made by multiplying the same number by itself, 3x3=9. There are many other strange and beautiful **number patterns**, some of which you will find out about in this book!

KEYPAD CRISIS

Play this with a friend.

**1** Oh no! You have been locked out of your spaceship and you need to get back inside! You need to press numbers on the keypads to let you back in, but some of the numbers are missing.

**2** Luckily all the numbers are laid out in patterns. But what are they?

**3** Some keypads have more than one number pattern. How many can you find?

**4** Look along the rows of numbers, up and down, and from corner to corner. You may be able to find more than one number pattern on the keypad. One player closes their eyes and the second player covers one number on each keypad.

**5** The first player opens their eyes and tries to figure out which number has been hidden.

# HELPFUL HINTS

● Some patterns are easy to follow. You can often figure them out by counting forward or counting backward. Which numbers come next in these sequences?

5  7  9  ?

21  18  15  12  ?

12  14  ?  18  20  22

● To find the missing number you needed to spot the number pattern.

● In these sequences there was a pattern of odd numbers, one which counted down in threes, and one of even numbers counting up in twos.

## MORE IDEAS

● You can make the keypad game more fun by hiding three or more numbers on each keypad.

● Try drawing your own keypad and making your own number patterns. If you are designing a pad to play against an adult, see how difficult you can make it!

# PATTERNS IN MULTIPLICATION

Knowing multiplication facts is very helpful when you are trying to solve some number problems. There are number patterns in multiplication that can help you remember your tables. You can also use your tables to make beautiful patterns.

## SPIROLATERALS

**1** You can make spirals with multiplication tables called spirolaterals. It helps to have some graph paper, but if you are careful with a ruler and a pencil, that will work too. Choose a multiplication table.

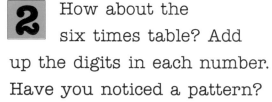

**2** How about the six times table? Add up the digits in each number. Have you noticed a pattern?

| 6 | 12 | 18 | 24 | 30 | 36 | 42 | 48 |
|---|----|----|----|----|----|----|----|
| 6 | 1+2 | 1+8 | 2+4 | 3+0 | 3+6 | 4+2 | 4+8 |
| 6 | 3 | 9 | 6 | 3 | 9 | 6 | 3 |

**because**
4+8=12
1+2=3

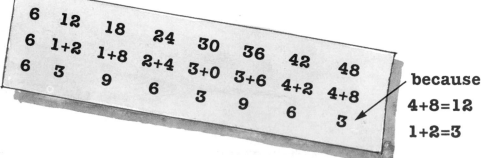

**3** If you get a two-digit number when you add the digits together, keep adding them until you get a single-digit number.

**4** Draw the first line 6 squares long then make a **right-angled** turn. The length of the next line is 3. Turn in the same direction again. The next is 9. Keep following the pattern until the lines start to retrace themselves. You could color in the patterns with colored pencils.

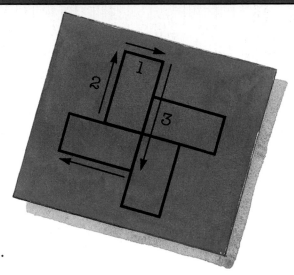

**5** Try doing the same with other multiplication tables. Do any look like these?

MORE IDEAS

● Tear the corner off a piece of cardboard. Draw a straight line from the corner to the torn edge. Cut along the line. Mark the top corner with an "x," mark points from the tip at 1, 2, and 3ins along the edge you have cut. On a plain piece of paper draw a line 2ins long. Place the cardboard along the line with corner "x" at one end. Draw a line 1in long back down the edge of the cardboard (using the measurements). Then rest your piece of cardboard along the line you have drawn with the marked corner at the end. Draw back 3ins along the measured edge. Repeat these three steps over and over until you have made a pattern like the one on the left.

# TRIANGULAR NUMBERS

Look at this number pattern

**1  3  6  10  15...**

What do you think comes next? This sequence is part of a special pattern called triangular numbers. To find out why they are called triangular numbers see page 212. It is made by adding consecutive numbers like this:

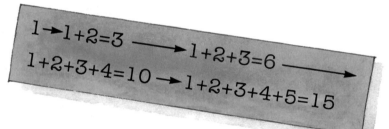

$1 \rightarrow 1+2=3 \longrightarrow 1+2+3=6 \longrightarrow$
$1+2+3+4=10 \rightarrow 1+2+3+4+5=15$

Use this pattern to advise the government of Metropolis!

## HIGHWAY MADNESS

**1** The government of Metropolis has decided to build highways to link their seven cities. Because they are worried about the environment, they make a rule that every city must be linked directly to every other city by only one road.

How many roads need to be built?

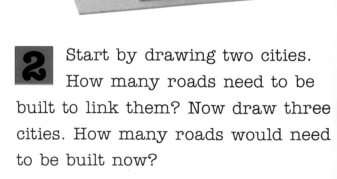

**2** Start by drawing two cities. How many roads need to be built to link them? Now draw three cities. How many roads would need to be built now?

**3** Without drawing out the highway system, predict how many highways would need to be built for the seven cities in Metropolis.

**4** Now mark them out and join them all with roads. Has the government of Metropolis made a good policy decision? What advice would you give to the government?

## HELPFUL HINTS

● First find out how many roads need to be built with a smaller number of cities – say 3, 4, and 5. Look at the pattern of the triangular numbers on page 212. Three cities need three roads (1+2=3). Four cities need six roads (1+2+3=6). You can use the triangular pattern to figure out how many roads five cities would need.

## MORE IDEAS

● Another interesting puzzle like Highway Madness is the handshakes problem. If you have eight people in a room and they all want to greet each other by shaking hands, how many handshakes will there be?

● You could start by figuring out how many handshakes you would need for a smaller group – as you did with the roads in Highway Madness.

# LETTERS AND NUMBERS

In mathematics letters are sometimes used to represent numbers. This branch of mathematics is called **algebra**. It is a useful way of solving problems when you don't have any numbers to help or you are not sure what the numbers might be. Sometimes the numbers can be found out, then they can be substituted into a formula. In other words, they are swapped over for some of the letters.

## NAME NUMBERS

**1** If a=1, b=2, c=3, and d=4, what do x, y, and z equal?

ANDREW is worth 65 points because
A=1   N=14   D=4   R=18   E=5   W=23
1 + 14 + 4 + 18 + 5 + 23 = 65

**2** How many points is your name worth?

Think about the names of friends. Whose name do you think is worth the most points? Is it the name with the most letters?

NICOLA = 54

**3** Do you have a "twin?" — someone whose name scores the same number of points as yours?

SIMON = 70

## HELPFUL HINTS

● When you are figuring out how much your name is worth, it is helpful to set all the letters of the alphabet out in a table so you can quickly look up their value.

● When you are adding up a lot of numbers, it is easy to make a mistake. Check what you have done. A calculator can be useful.

MORE IDEAS

● The title of this page is "Letters and Numbers." It is worth 210 points. Can you make a sentence that is worth 200 points? How close can you get?

Can you score 300 points using a 17-letter sentence?

# OPERATIONS AND FUNCTIONS

A function is when +, −, x, ÷, or other operations are used to change numbers. A **function** is a little like a machine in a factory that processes, or changes, something into something else.

## NUMBER CRUNCHERS

**1** You are the new engineer in the factory. You can see how the machine below works because the machine's functions are clearly labeled on the outside. When the 3 goes in, a 7 comes out because the function inside is x2 and then +1.

**2** Unfortunately not all the machines are as clearly labeled. But you discover that if you put a number in a machine, it still gets crunched and changed.

$$3 \rightarrow \boxed{x2} \quad \boxed{+1} \rightarrow 7$$

Test the machine a few more times. What would happen if you put a number 6 in? What about 23? Try some other numbers and see what happens.

**3** Try finding out the function for this number cruncher!

Which functions do you think were used in the big machine to turn the 2 into a 4? Can you think of any other way of doing it?

# HELPFUL HINTS

● If you get stuck, try out a few operations in the machines and see what happens when you put a number in. Look for a pattern.

● If you are really stuck here are some clues:

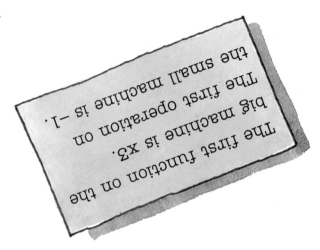

The first function on the big machine is ×3. The first operation on the small machine is −1.

MORE IDEAS

● Make up your own number cruncher machines. You could have more than two operations in each machine! Figure out some inputs and outputs, then see if a friend can solve your puzzle!

# 5 THINK OF A NUMBER

In algebra, when letters are used in calculations they could mean anything! But we can still work with them. If we do not know what a number is we could call it "n." Here is a trick that will work with any number. Try it out on your friends.

n

×6

×3

-18

## NUMBER RECYCLING PLANT

**1** This is a way of calculating with any number and changing it using lots of different operations – adding, multiplying, dividing, and subtracting – and always arriving at the same result!

**2** Your friends may need a calculator and a pencil and paper to help them.

**Divide by the number you first thought of.**

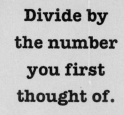

**3** Now say to your friends, "This truly remarkable trick can magically transform any number into a beautiful single one! Yes, it is true!"

## HELPFUL HINTS

● Make sure you remember the number you started with. It helps to keep a note of your calculations.

● This could be recorded in a table:

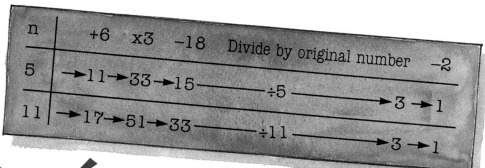

| n |  | +6 | x3 | −18 | Divide by original number | −2 |  |
|---|---|---|---|---|---|---|---|
| 5 | →11 | →33 | →15 | | ÷5 | →3 | →1 |
| 11 | →17 | →51 | →33 | | ÷11 | →3 | →1 |

● Can you see now how the trick works?

## MORE IDEAS

● If you divide any number by itself, the answer is always 1. 7÷7=1, 5÷5=1, 59÷59=1, and 123÷123=1. Try doing the same with another number.

● Now you know how the magic works, try to make your own trick using many different functions that can turn numbers into ones.

● What happens when you divide or multiply a number by 0? Could you use this in your trick?

**4** Choose a number from one to a hundred, follow the operations, and presto!... one.

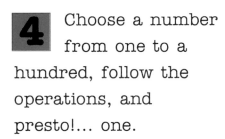

# NUMBER CODES

We are so used to counting with the numerals 0123456789 and using the decimal system that they seem timeless, as though they have always been there. But they haven't! Different cultures have used a variety of counting systems and numbers.

Some of these can still be seen in regular use. Have you seen any Roman numerals? Letters are used to represent the numbers.

I V X L C D M
1 5 10 50 100 500 1000

= 0    = 1

= 2    = 3

= 4

The Mayan people lived over 2,000 years ago. Their number system used twenties and ones. We need to decode the system to know what the symbols represent.

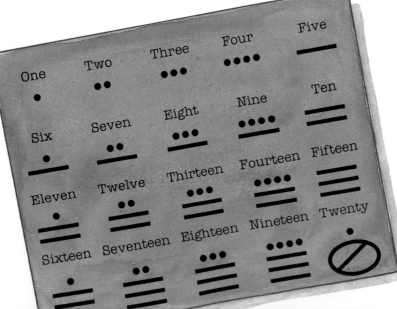

One Two Three Four Five

Six Seven Eight Nine Ten

Eleven Twelve Thirteen Fourteen Fifteen

Sixteen Seventeen Eighteen Nineteen Twenty

A number like 57 would be written like this...
**because**
  **2x20=40**
  **+17=57**

Twenties

Ones

## NUMBER DISCOVERY

**1** Imagine that you have been exploring uncharted land. You stumble across a stone tablet. There are some strange markings – they look like numbers.

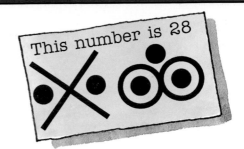

This number is 28

=5 =6

=7 =8

=9

You eventually figure out what each symbol means.

**2** What number do you think this is?

**3** How would you write down 82? What about 56? Try 170!

Answer is 7 1 5

### MORE IDEAS

● Make up some problems with the numbers and see if your friends can solve them.

● Can you make up your own number codes?

● Find out about other counting systems. The Babylonian system is amazing!

The system of counting was based on fives from 1 – 19 and then in groups of twenty.

This symbol represented a zero.

# KNOW YOUR NUMBERS

The more you know about numbers the more patterns, links, and connections you will be able to make between them. What do you know about the number **25**? It is a square number, because **5x5=25**. It is a quarter of **100**. My uncle is **25** years old. It is an odd number. List everything you know about another number. How many connections can you make?

A solo spot for me. Odd and on my own. Who am I?

I had 10 subtracted and then I was multiplied by 2. That made 12. Who am I?

I can be divided by 12, 9, 6, 4, 3, and 2. If I am multiplied by 10 the answer is the same as the degrees in a whole turn. I am an even number. The product of my digits is 18. Who am I?

I was multiplied by 3 and then 3 was added. That made 30. Who am I?

The number of squares on a chessboard. 2 multiplied by itself six times. Who am I?

## MYSTERY NUMBERS

**1** The more you know about numbers the easier it will be for you to solve these number riddles. What are the mystery numbers and how are they all connected?

76

The sum of the first five odd numbers. An odd two digit number. Who am I?

The sum of my digits is said to be unlucky. I am not quite half a century. Who am I?

Add the sides of a square to the faces on a die and multiply by 10. Who am I?

I was divided by 9 and when 8 was subtracted, I was cut down to the size of just 1. Who am I?

The legs on most animals, tables, and chairs. Who am I?

# HELPFUL HINTS

● With some of the mystery numbers you can work backward to find the answer by using the inverse or opposite operation. The inverse of x3 is ÷3.

The inverse of +6 is −6.

● For the problem "I was multiplied by 3 and then 3 was added. That made 30. Who am I?" you can begin from the 30. Work backward by subtracting 3, which makes 27 and then dividing by 3, which gives 9... the answer!

## MORE IDEAS

● Make up your own mystery numbers! Think up your clues carefully and try them out on your friends. Remember to check your clues first!

# MORE MYSTERY

To solve some problems you have to try to keep in mind a number of clues at the same time – simultaneously. In fact these are sometimes called simultaneous equations. They can be solved algebraically, but many simple ones can also be solved through trial and error. Try these!

## COMBINATION CRACKERS

You have been on the trail of cunning criminals who have stolen some valuable jewels! A tattered, smudged piece of paper has been secretly passed to you with some clues that enable you to unlock the case holding the treasure.

**1** The case has a four-digit combination lock and you only have a matter of minutes before the thieves return.

These are the clues...

The third digit is three more than the first.

The second digit is two more than the fourth.

All the digits add up to 17.

The second digit is three.

# HELPFUL HINTS

● Stuck?! Then try to solve the problem using algebra. If the digits are a, b, c, and d, we know that b=d+2 and that b=3. So if b=3 then 3=d+2 and therefore d=1.

● Use algebra to find out what a and c are. When the numbers you have chosen match all the clues then you have cracked the code and unlocked the case!

Answer is 5 3 8 1

## MORE IDEAS

● If you found the first puzzle easy try this one!

You need to escape on a high-powered motorcycle, but it is chained up by, would you believe it, a four-digit combination lock. These are your clues for unlocking it...

● Why don't you find your own chain or case and make up your own clues!

The motorcycle answer is 3 1 6 4

**The first number is one less than the fourth.**

**The sum of all the digits is fourteen.**

**The third number is twice as big as the first.**

**The fourth number is two less than the third.**

# MAN-MADE PATTERNS

People love patterns. Patterns can be seen all over the world on buildings, on furniture, clothes, and even on bodies. Have you seen any ancient Celtic knot patterns or those created by Islamic artists across the Middle East and North Africa? Perhaps you know of others. These designs illustrate many beautiful mathematical patterns.

## SHONGO PATTERNS

This intricate pattern comes from Africa and is drawn by children on the ground in mud, clay, or sand.

**1** The pattern is drawn in one continuous line. Your pencil should never be lifted from the paper. You can cross lines, but you should never go along the same line twice.

1st   Start

Finish

**2** These are the first three patterns in the sequence. Try to draw them.

2nd

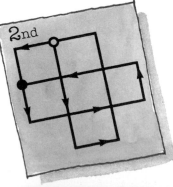

3rd

**3** When you have drawn the first three try to draw the fourth. What about the fifth? Remember, your pencil should never leave the paper.

**4** What patterns do you notice as you draw the shapes?

How long is the starting line on each of the new shapes? Count the squares covered by each shape. Can you see any number patterns?

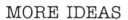

Describe as much as you can about the 100th shongo pattern without any drawing.

# HELPFUL HINTS

● If you find it hard to get a sense of the pattern, trace over the shapes following the arrows on the lines carefully.

● It is a good idea to start drawing the patterns on graph paper. As you become more confident draw the shapes freehand on blank paper.

● After a little practice, you will be surprised how quickly they can be drawn.

● When you are looking for patterns, it is a good idea to note what you see in a table.

| Shape | 1st | 2nd | 3rd | 4th |
|---|---|---|---|---|
| Perimeter | 8 | 12 | 16 | |

## MORE IDEAS

● This beautiful pattern comes from an ancient Celtic gravestone.

● Find some patterns from other cultures and try to draw them.

● What similarities or differences are there between the patterns you have found and the shongo pattern?

# NATURAL PATTERNS

Nature is full of patterns. Next time you look at a plant or tree in your yard or park look at the curves, **angles**, and spirals that are formed. These patterns can be represented by numbers.

SPIRALS
You can draw many of these patterns by following a series of simple instructions.

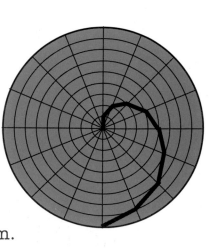

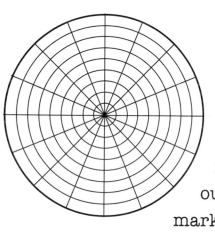

**1** Follow the instructions in Helpful Hints to help you make this circular grid. Starting from the center, move out to the first ring and mark a point.

**2** Lift your pen and move one section of the grid clockwise and out to the next circle and mark the point. Join the points.

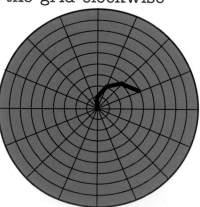

Keep moving out and clockwise one circle at a time, marking points and joining them.

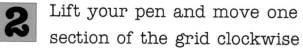

**3** When you reach the outside circle, you will have made a curve.

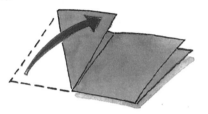

# HELPFUL HINTS

● Find a piece of graph paper. Keep your compass point in the middle and draw 10 circles a half inch apart. Fold the paper in half and fold each side over and then over again.

## MORE IDEAS

● Make another curve starting from the same center point. This time turn counterclockwise. You have drawn a beautiful leaf. Make lots of curves in a pattern on the same grid.

● Try other patterns. What happens if you move out two circles at a time?

● Try moving out one circle and turning two sectors.

● Other patterns can be made by following the grid lines and coloring in bright colors rather than just joining the points.

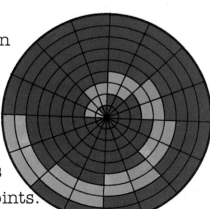

# NATURAL NUMBERS

Nature can change simple number patterns into beautiful shapes. The Fibonacci sequence can be found everywhere in nature. Artists and architects have also used it in designs. It begins like this **1 1 2 3 5 8 13 21 34...** Can you see what the pattern is? The next number in the sequence is created by adding the previous two numbers, so the next number will be 21+34=55.

## FIBONACCI FACTS

Did you know that the number of clockwise spirals on a sunflower head is 55 and the counterclockwise spirals is 34? Count them and check! Pineapples have 8 seeds arranged in a clockwise spiral and 13 in a counterclockwise spiral.

## CURVE STITCHING

Other beautiful patterns can be made by adding numbers. For this project you will need a thick piece of cardboard. Draw out a cross on it.

**1** On each arm of the cross mark five points 1in apart. Mark the points on each arm with the numbers 1, 2, 3, 4, and 5. Pierce each point with a thick needle. Get an adult to help you with this.

**2** Thread a needle with a long piece of yarn. Choose your favorite color. In one quarter, stitch together the points that add up to 6, for example 1 and 5. When you have done one quarter, move on to the next with a different color yarn.

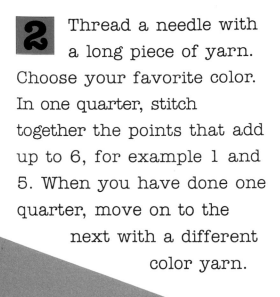

## MORE IDEAS

● Try dividing consecutive numbers in the Fibonacci sequence. A calculator is useful for doing this! Start by trying 8÷5=1.6. You will discover that the larger the numbers you divide, the closer you will get to approximately 1.618... This figure is known as The Golden Ratio. This ratio 1:1.6 has been used to design buildings like the ancient Greek Parthenon on the Acropolis.

● Take any four consecutive numbers in the Fibonacci pattern, for example 2, 3, 5, and 8. Multiply the two outside numbers (2x8=16). Multiply the two inside numbers (3x5=15). Subtract the second number from the first. Whichever four consecutive numbers you choose, if you follow this calculation, the answer will always be 1.

● Here is the sequence in reverse. What do you think comes next?

8 5 3 2 1 1 0 1 –1....

# CONTENTS

# Chapter Four

# Getting the Facts

# SORTING AND SETS

When your mom or dad says "clean your room!" they are really just trying to help you with your mathematics! When you clean up, you may group and order your toys so they can be found more easily. Each group of toys is called a **set**. Every toy is called an **element**.

## THESE SHOES ARE MADE FOR WALKING

You can do this with a brother, sister, or friend.

**1** How many shoes are there in the house? Ask an adult if you can collect them all together and put them in one big pile.

**2** This is the set of all shoes in the house. Each shoe is an element of the set. How many shoes are there in the set? Let's hope it is an even number!

**3** Find two colored towels. Sort the shoes into two sets on the towels: adult's shoes and children's shoes. Each of these groups is called a subset.

**4** Can you sort them in any other way?

Dress shoes and everyday shoes.

Indoor and outdoor shoes.

Uncomfortable and comfortable shoes.

Left foot and right foot shoes.

Shoes that are smaller than your foot and shoes that are larger.

**5** Sort them into sets that belong to each person in the house.

**6** And last of all, can you sort them so that they go back to the right place in the house?

# CARROLL DIAGRAMS

A set of elements have at least one thing, or **property**, in common. If you have a set of fruit you can say that any element in the set is either "an apple" or "not an apple." Carroll diagrams are a way of sorting information like this.

PICK 'N' MIX

Have you ever opened a large box of candy and then spent a long time looking for your favorite... or avoided the one with the chewy center that you hate! A Carroll diagram can help you to sort out the yummy from the yucky. First decide on something about the candy you really like... perhaps you like toffee... perhaps you hate chocolate.

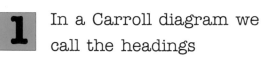

**1** In a Carroll diagram we call the headings **categories**. In this diagram toffee and chocolate will be the categories. Draw your diagram like the one at the top of page 91.

A candy that has toffee and chocolate would go here.

| | Chocolate | Not chocolate |
|---|---|---|
| Toffee | | |
| Not toffee | | |

One that has chocolate but no toffee would go here.

Where would you put a candy that has no chocolate and no toffee?

**2** Sort out your candy. In which part of the diagram are your favorite candy? Where are your least favorite?

# HELPFUL HINTS

● Most candy boxes give a guide to their contents on the side. Keep it handy. It might stop you from making a terrible mistake!

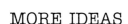

## MORE IDEAS
● What else can you sort using Carroll diagrams? How about the laundry? (Ask an adult.)
● Try categories like "shirt" and "not shirt," and "adult" and "not adult."

# VENN DIAGRAMS

The elements of a set don't always fall into two easy groups. An element might be a part of different sets at the same time. Venn diagrams are a useful way of showing this.

DOUBLE TROUBLE!
This is a game that uses a Venn diagram. Pick a subject for your set. What about animals?

**1** Draw two overlapping circles as below, or make them from colored cardboard. Label each circle as a different subset.

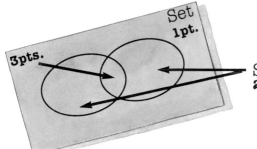

Set
1pt.

3pts.

Subsets
2pts.

ANIMALS
CARNIVOROUS
LION
T.REX
SABER TOOTH
STEGO-SAURUS
MOO
PREMISTORIC

**2** You might choose prehistoric and carnivorous animals. Each circle is a subset of the whole (universal) set of animals.

**3** Think of any animal. Write it on a piece of cardboard and place it where it belongs on the diagram. A Stegosaur scores two points, a cow scores one point.

**4** What about a carnivorous (meat-eating) animal? A lion scores two points.

**5** If you can think of an animal that is carnivorous and prehistoric it would go in the striped intersection and score three points!

## HELPFUL HINTS

● It might be useful to find books with animal facts and dinosaur facts to help you play this game.

## MORE IDEAS

● You could make up your own game using other sets. How about the set of musical instruments. The two overlapping subsets could be electrical instruments and stringed instruments!

● Harder, but great fun, is to think up three overlapping sets. Try this one. How would you change the scoring system?

Animals with fur

Carnivorous animals

Animals that live in water

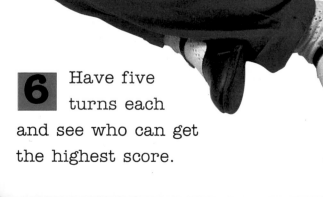

**6** Have five turns each and see who can get the highest score.

# THINKING LOGICALLY

When you woke up this morning you solved quite a tricky problem – getting dressed! You had to think logically. What did you do first? What did you do next? Did you put your clothes on in the correct order and on the right parts of your body?!

THE SHOWMAN, HIS TIGER, A DUCK, AND THE SACK OF CORN

How good are you at thinking logically? This is an old problem. You need to help the showman cross a river with his tiger, duck, and sack of corn.

**1** There is a boat but it is so small that it can only hold the showman and one of the others.

**2** The showman can't leave the tiger with the duck as the duck will be eaten. He can't leave the duck with the corn for fear of losing all the corn. How does he get across?

**3** Find some toys and pretend they are the showman, tiger, duck, and corn. Make a river with blue paper.

**4** Put all the toys on one side of the river. What would happen if the showman took the tiger over first? Is it a better plan to take the corn? Would it be a good idea to take the duck?

CORN

**5** When you think you have figured out how it could be done, make up a short story with the toys and tell it to your friends.

# HELPFUL HINTS

● Have you worked out the first thing that the showman should transport across the river?

● It couldn't be the tiger, because the duck would be left on its own with the tasty corn!

● He couldn't take the corn because the tiger would be all alone with the juicy duck!! So, the first thing that needs to go is the... duck.

● What happens next? One last clue: The showman can bring something back across the river with him if he needs to.

## MORE IDEAS

● The Towers of Hanoi is an ancient logic problem. You need to move the pile of disks from the red square to the green square. Only one disk may be moved at a time. A larger disk can never be placed on a smaller disk. You could play this game with three coins of different sizes. What is the smallest number of moves it takes to do it?

# PLAY TO WIN!

Have you ever played Tic-tac-toe? Can anyone beat you? If you play cleverly, you can make sure that you never lose! To play this game well you need to use logic. There are many games that depend on skill and strategy (planning). Chess and Checkers are good games; perhaps you could also find out about Othello or Go.

DIAMONDS
Diamonds is an ancient game of skill for two players that some believe was played by Arabian princes.

**1** First you need to make a square board divided into 16 squares. Cut out 20 counters, you could make them diamond-shaped.

**2** When you play Tic-tac-toe you need to get a line of three to win. But in Diamonds you lose if three diamonds are placed in a line. The line might be vertical, horizontal, diagonal, even if there is a gap in the line.

**3** Each player has 10 diamonds. Take turns to place a diamond on a square.

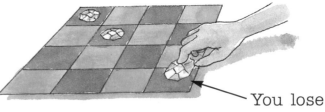

You lose

# HELPFUL HINTS

● Before you put a diamond on the board look carefully! Check each row and don't forget the diagonal lines.

**4** The winner takes all the diamonds on the board! Start the game again and play with your new set of diamonds. The game ends when one person has won all the diamonds.

## MORE IDEAS

● What is the greatest number of diamonds you could fit on the board without getting three in a straight line? It is easy to place 6. Can you fit on any more?

● It is fun to try this game on a 64-square chessboard. You can play with up to six players!

# THE RIGHT PLACE

Finding the right place to send, store, or find things can be a tricky business. Look at the address on some letters that have been sent to you. Your address might have a house number, street name, the town you live in, state, zip code, and perhaps country, – lots of information to make sure that the letter reaches the right person.

AMAZING MONSTER MOUNTAINS.
Use colored cardboard, pens, and glue to make the monsters and mountain in the picture.

**1** Are you brave enough to help them find their home on the mountain?

**2** Here are some clues to help you.

- All the monsters on the right of the mountain have round, green bodies. The other monsters have red bodies.

- Monsters at the bottom of the mountain have short, green hair. All the other monsters have blue, curly hair.

- The monsters all have two eyes except the one at the peak that has three.

- All of the monsters on the mountain have triangular noses, two feet, and two arms.

**3** Some of the places on the mountain are still empty. You might have to make some more monsters and put them in their homes.

# HELPFUL HINTS

- When you are deciding where to put your monster check against all the clues one at a time. Then go through the clues and make a list of the different things you need to include in your drawing. Your list might look something like this:

green body
blue, curly hair
two eyes

## MORE IDEAS

- You can make more great monster mountain puzzles with your friends. Draw a mountain, or trace the one on the page. Add more features like a cave or some trees.

- Next, make up some clues, then draw the monsters. Make sure they match the clues you have given!

# DEFINITELY MAYBE

Do you think it will rain tomorrow? If you take a card from a deck what are the chances you will draw an ace? When mathematicians study questions like these they are studying the likelihood or probability of something happening.

## FLIPPER

When you flip a coin into the air what might happen when it lands? Two things could happen. It might show a head or a tail. The likelihood of getting a tail is one chance in two, or you could say a half.

**1** This is a game for three players. You need two different coins, a pencil, and some squared graph paper to keep score.

**2** The first player gets a point if you can see two heads after the coins have been flipped. The second player gets a point if you can see a head and a tail.

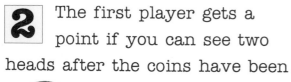

The third player gets a point if there are two tails.

**3** Take turns to be the coin flipper and keep score of the points.

**4** Flip the coins about 20 times each. Who is winning? Is this a fair game? Which team would you rather be if you started the game again?

# HELPFUL HINTS

● It makes it easier to understand this game if you use two different coins when you are flipping. You can find out which team has the best chance of winning by looking at all the possible things that could happen – the possible outcomes. There are four possibilities:

**Coin 1** **Coin 2**

● There is only one chance in four of getting two heads and only one chance in four of getting two tails, but there are two chances in four of getting one of each!

● What are you going to choose next time?

## MORE IDEAS

● Try playing Flipper with four coins. Which would be the best "team" to choose? All heads? How about two heads and two tails? Do you think three tails and a head would be best? Experiment, find out, then challenge your friends to a game!

● Why is "heads I win, tails you lose" an unfair way to decide who wins when you flip a coin?

# TAKE A CHANCE

There are many games that use a mixture of luck, skill, and strategy. Backgammon is an exciting game to play, so is Monopoly. Good players are those that know how to make the best decision whatever the throw of the die or draw of the cards. Can you work out the best way to play Sweaty palms?

## SWEATY PALMS

**1** You need some dried beans and three or more players for this game – in fact the more players you have the better! Each player secretly holds one or two beans in his or her hand.

**2** Next, everyone tries to guess the total being held by the whole group. The person who makes the best guess is the winner!

**3** How many beans do you think these four players are holding? Is 3 a good guess? Are some guesses better than others?

**4** Play the game a few times. Do some numbers come up more often than others? What are your chances of making a correct guess?

## HELPFUL HINTS

● Be careful when you make your guess.

● Remember that each player must hold one or two beans. If everyone is holding one what is the total being held? If everyone is holding two what is the total being held now?

### MORE IDEAS

● To get really good at Sweaty palms look at all the different ways the numbers could be made in a game with four players. How many ways are there of making 4? What about 8? Can you figure out how many ways there are of making the other possible numbers: 5, 6, and 7?

● The number that can be made the most different ways is the best choice!

# SPIN THE SPINNER

Many games of chance depend on the roll of a die or a spin of a disk. Can you think of some? When a die is rolled there are six possible outcomes – either a 1, 2, 3, 4, 5, or 6.

## SIX-A-SIDE SOCCER SPIN

**1** Have you ever played five-a-side soccer? This is a game of six-a-side with spinners! You need to make one spinner for every person playing. You will need cardboard, scissors, and some pens or pencils. Each player must choose a team from the grid below.

**2** Pick a team from the grid below. Each team has its own numbers.

| Team | Numbers on spinner | | | | | |
|------|------|------|------|------|------|------|
| Amazing Aces | 1 | 2 | 3 | 4 | 5 | 6 |
| Burning Bulls | 5 | 2 | 3 | 3 | 4 | 4 |
| Crazy Cavaliers | 0 | 0 | 6 | 5 | 6 | 7 |
| Eazy Eagles | 2 | 5 | 5 | 1 | 2 | 5 |

**3** Cut the cardboard into a six-sided regular hexagon like this. Draw and decorate your team's spinner with the numbers and colors and push a sharp pencil through the center.

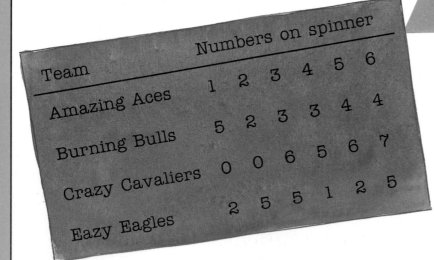

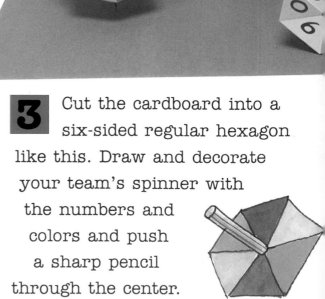

**4** To play a match against another team, spin the spinner. The spinner that comes to rest on the highest number wins the match.

**6** Play ten matches against each team. Don't count the draws. Which team did you choose? Why did you think it had the best chance of winning? If you played again, would you choose the same team?

**5** If your team is the Cavaliers and four of you are playing then you might keep a scorecard like this:

| Cavaliers | | |
|---|---|---|
| | 6-4 | |
| Cavaliers | | Eagles |
| | 3-7 | |
| Cavaliers | | Aces |
| | | |
| Cavaliers | | Bulls |

## HELPFUL HINTS

● You can find out which teams are the best by working out all the possible outcomes when two of the spinners are spun. You could make a color chart to compare the Cavaliers and the Aces:

| Cavaliers | | | | | | |
|---|---|---|---|---|---|---|
| 7 | C | C | C | C | C | C |
| 6 | C | C | C | C | C | D |
| 5 | C | C | C | C | D | A |
| 6 | C | C | C | C | C | D |
| 0 | A | A | A | A | A | A |
| 0 | A | A | A | A | A | A |
| | 1 | 2 | 3 | 4 | 5 | 6 |

**Aces**

● There are 36 possible outcomes. There are 20 possibilities that the Cavaliers could win (red), 3 of a draw (yellow), and 13 for the Aces to win (blue). So, the Cavaliers have a better team.

# GRAPHS AND CHARTS

**Graphs** and charts are used by mathematicians to make information clearer or make certain facts stand out. If you were collecting information to find your friends' favorite cartoon character you might begin by keeping a check list. But you can show this information more clearly in a bar graph.

## THE TOP TEN CHART

You could use a bar graph to help plan the music for a party. You would need to find out the type of music that everyone would want to dance to. What information do you need to help you decide? What are your friends' favorite pop stars? First, draw out a tally table like the one on the left.

**1** Now ask your friends to name three pop stars they like. Write down each name mentioned and put a check by it each time that name gets a vote.

**2** Next, draw out a bar graph using the information you collected in your check list. Each pop star gets one colored square for each vote. You can use your graph to find out which pop music is favorite!

# HELPFUL HINTS

● You might find it easier to use graph paper when you are filling in your bar graph. Make sure the paper is long enough to fit in the pop star with the most checks. If you don't plan carefully you might run out of room at the top of the graph!

Pop Star C

Pop Star D

Pop Star E

## MORE IDEAS

● Another graph like a bar graph is a pictogram. Instead of coloring in a block, draw a small picture of each item that gets a vote. You could use a pictogram to plan the food at your party. Collect information about what everyone likes to eat and try to chart the information in a pictogram.

# DATASTREAMS

Some information gathered in experiments is continuous! When you are young your growth is continuous – it doesn't stop. If you measured your height every year you could make a graph of the data. It may look like there are sudden big jumps in the graph but in fact you did grow continuously over the year.

## UPS AND DOWNS

Have you ever taken part in an important event like a school play? Throughout the day you might sometimes feel happy and at other times sad. A datastream is a good way of showing this.

**1** Look at this graph. It shows the feelings of someone taking part in a school play, from when she wakes up in the morning to when the performance finishes.

**2** The graph has been written on (or annotated) to describe why she felt happy or sad at different times.

**Wake up and remember play**

**Happy**

**Go to school**

**Sad**

**Eat horrible lunch**

**Finish work before play**

8.00

10.00

12.00

2.00

4.00

**3** Choose your own special event and draw out a graph like this one.

**Prepare costume for play**

**Play starts**

**Audience claps**

**Forget my lines**

**4** Next, annotate the graph to help describe why you felt either happy or sad at different times in the day.

00

8.00

# HELPFUL HINTS

● You could start the graph by drawing a horizontal line across the page.

● Mark a point on the left and, next to it, the time you woke up. Now draw a vertical line straight up.

● Write in the time on the horizontal line. You might find it easier  to think about how you felt at the time you woke up, then mark a point; how you felt when you got to school, then mark a point. Mark points throughout the day and finally join up the points to make a curve.

## MORE IDEAS

● Sometimes when you take part in an exciting event you might not feel just happy or sad. You could feel a mixture of both feelings – at the end of the play you could feel happy that everyone thought you had done well, but sad that the play had finished. How could you show that on the graph?

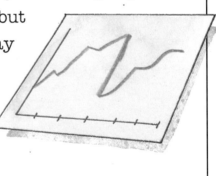

# A PIECE OF PIE!

Many types of graphs and charts are used to show information clearly. Pie charts are usually circle-shaped. They are used to show fractions of a whole. Why do you think it is called a pie chart? This pie chart shows how children traveled to their school. Which part of the pie is the largest? It is easy to see that most children walked to school.

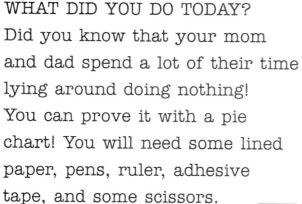

## WHAT DID YOU DO TODAY?

Did you know that your mom and dad spend a lot of their time lying around doing nothing! You can prove it with a pie chart! You will need some lined paper, pens, ruler, adhesive tape, and some scissors.

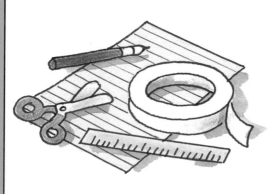

**1** First you need to gather some information. Ask your mom or dad how much time every day they spend on eating, the amount of time at work, time spent watching T.V., the amount of time traveling, and the amount of time sleeping.

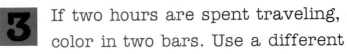

**2** Next, cut out a long bar from the lined paper about 5 inches wide stretching over 24 lines. Each line represents one hour of the day.

**3** If two hours are spent traveling, color in two bars. Use a different color for each activity. When you have filled in the 24 bars loop the strip over into a circle and stick the ends together. Rest the circle on some paper, draw around it, and mark off the points for each activity. Draw a line from the points to the center and color in the different sections.

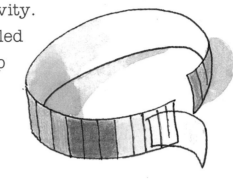

## HELPFUL HINTS

● When you are collecting your information the time doesn't need to be exact. Measurements to the nearest hour or half hour will do.

## MORE IDEAS

● You can use pie charts to find the amount of time a T.V. channel gives to different types of programs. Look at a T.V. guide and choose a channel. How much time is given to news, cartoons, movies, or other categories? Turn the information into a pie chart.

# CONTENTS

# Chapter Five

# Exploring Shapes

# SQUARES AND RECTANGLES

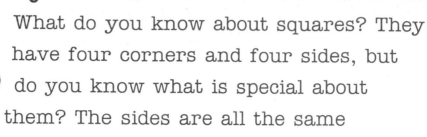

What do you know about squares? They have four corners and four sides, but do you know what is special about them? The sides are all the same length and the angles at the corners are all the same. Rectangles' corners are all the same angle and their opposite sides are the same length.

## THE BLACK HOLE

**1** Two players must try to cover a piece of paper with rectangles, without falling down the black hole! You need paper, colored pencils, and a ruler.

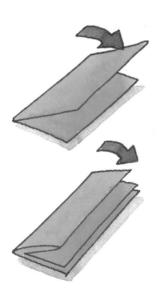

**2** To make the grid for the game, fold a piece of paper in half lengthways as shown in the picture. Repeat this three more times. Unfold the paper and do the same, folding from top to bottom.

**3** Unfold the paper and draw lines along the folds to make your grid. Choose any square and draw the black hole.

**4** Players take turns to color a rectangle following the lines of the grid. You could draw a rectangle that takes up lots of spaces or one that takes up just one space if you like. Avoid the black hole. If you draw over the black hole you lose!

## HELPFUL HINTS

● A ruler might help you to draw the sides of the rectangle straight.

● You can draw a square on the grid because a square is a rectangle, too!

## MORE IDEAS

● If you are good at playing The Black Hole, try Sea Monsters!

● Make the grid again, but this time draw four sea monsters on it.

● Can you draw rectangles that avoid the hungry beasts?

# TESSELLATIONS

Do you have any tiles in your house? There might be some in the kitchen or bathroom, on the walls, or on the floor. The tiles are often square shaped because they fit together easily, leaving no gaps. When a shape fits together like this we say the shape tessellates.

## TESSELLATING TILES

You can use squares to make interesting tessellating shapes. You will need some paper, thick cardboard, a compass, tape, scissors, a pencil, and colored markers.

**1** Cut a square of cardboard with sides of about 2in.

**2** Cut out a part of the square and move the part to the opposite side of the square like this.

**3** Attach it to the other side of the square with some tape. Place your new tile in the middle of the paper and draw around it lightly with a pencil.

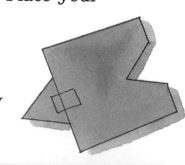

**4** Pick up the tile and place it so it fits in with the first outline. There shouldn't be any gaps! Keep repeating this across the page until it is covered.

**5** Outline the tiles with a thick marker and decorate the tiles with a bright pattern.

# HELPFUL HINTS

● You can make a square with a compass. Open the arms about 2in apart. Place the point at the corner of the page (A) and make a mark with the compass along the two edges of the paper (B and C). Place the compass point on B and mark an arc, do the same on C. Where the arcs cross mark D. Use the ruler to join A, B, C, and D and cut out your square.

## MORE IDEAS

● Try making more complex tile patterns by cutting out more than one part of the square.

● Make sure you move the part you have cut to line up exactly on the opposite side of the square.

# THE THIRD DIMENSION

Shapes that are flat, like squares and rectangles, have two **dimensions**, length and width. Three-dimensional shapes, like cereal boxes and cans, also have height. Some boxes can be opened out and flattened. When this is done you can see the two-dimensional shapes, called faces, it is made from. The flat unfolded shape is the **net** of the box.

## FISHING NETS

Find a die. How many faces does it have? What shape are they? There are six square faces. We call this shape a cube. If you could unfold the cube to make a net what would it look like?

**1** Make six equal squares from cardboard — these will be the six faces of the cube. Draw a fishing net and fish on each of the faces.

**2** Arrange the squares with one or more of their sides together to make a net for a cube. If your net were folded, would it make a cube?

**3** Tape the squares on the plain sides and try folding the net into a cube. Does it work? If it does, unfold it again and draw a picture of the arrangement of the squares.

**4** Can you find another way of arranging the squares into a net that makes a cube?

# HELPFUL HINTS

● A quick way of making a large square is to take the corner of a piece of thin cardboard and bend it over until it reaches the opposite side like this.

● Make a mark where it meets the edge then fold the small piece over so that a straight line is made across the cardboard. Cut along the line to make the square.

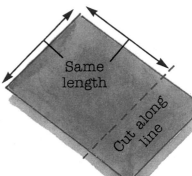

Same length

Cut along line

## MORE IDEAS

● Draw some nets that you know can be folded to make a cube. Now draw some nets that you know will not make a cube.

● Challenge your friends to figure out just by looking at the nets whether they will make a cube.

**5** There are lots of different nets that make a cube. How many can you find?

# TRIANGLES

I'm sure you know what a triangle is but did you know how amazing they are? You can use them to make many shapes with any number of straight sides. Take these triangles for a "walk" and see what shapes you can make!

## WALKING TRIANGLES

**1** Draw a triangle with a ruler on a piece of cardboard. Cut it out carefully. Mark one of the corners with a marker on the front and back.

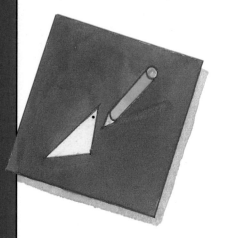

**2** Put your triangle on a piece of paper. The marked corner stays fixed — it does not ever move from that spot. Draw around the triangle.

**3** Now, flip over the triangle, keeping the marked point fixed and the edge of the outline touching the cardboard like this. Draw around the triangle again.

**4** Keep repeating this until the triangles you have drawn are about to overlap. Draw around the edge of your shape with a ruler and color in the triangles carefully to make some beautiful patterns.

## HELPFUL HINTS

● When you draw around your triangle, do it lightly and quickly with a pencil. If you make a mistake, it is easy to erase it later. Remember, you will be going over the lines later with markers and a ruler.

## MORE IDEAS

● Don't stop drawing the triangles when they are about to overlap.

Keep walking the triangle! What happens to the shape that you make? Go on, get carried away!

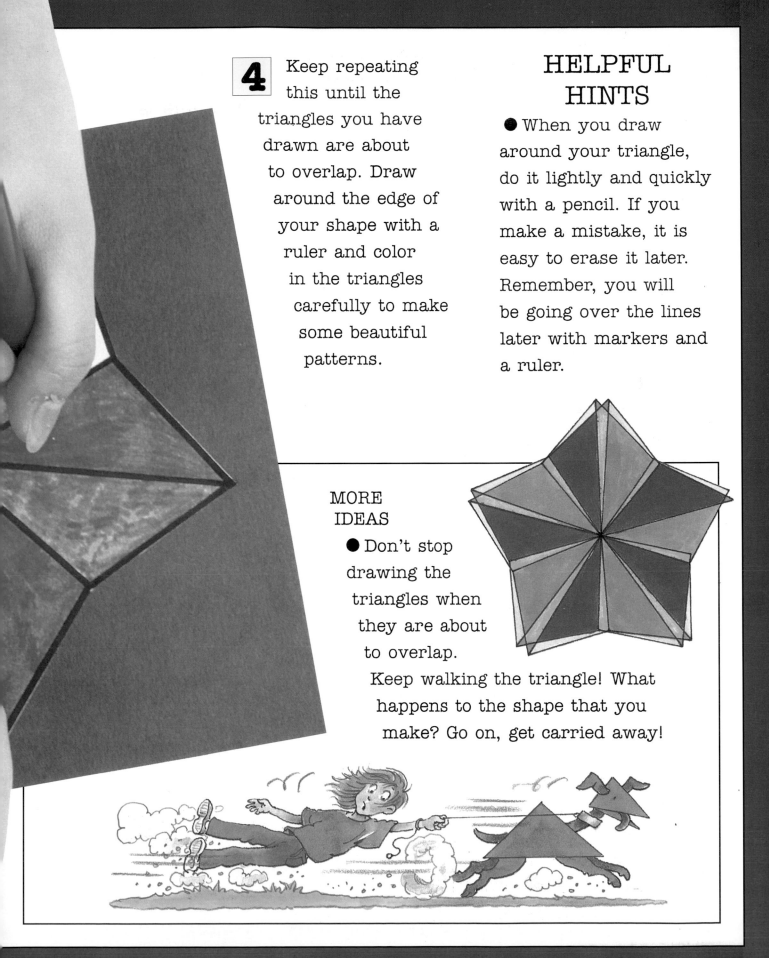

# MORE TRIANGLES

Did you know there are different types of triangles?

An isosceles triangle has two sides of equal length — the marks show that sides are equal.

All the sides of an equilateral triangle are the same length.

A right-angled triangle has one corner that looks like the corner of a square.

A scalene triangle has no equal sides.

## TROTTO!

**1** Trotto can be played by two, three, or four players. To play, make 12 cards. On each card draw a triangle, make sure you draw three of each type. Draw in the marks on the equilateral, isosceles, and right-angled triangles.

**2** Find a die and cover each face with blank stickers. Write "miss turn" twice, "scalene," "isosceles," "equilateral," "right-angled" on the faces.

**3** Deal out the cards. Place them on the floor face up. Take turns to throw the die. If it shows one of your triangles turn it over and pass the die to the next player.

**4** The winner is the first player to turn over all their cards!

# HELPFUL HINTS

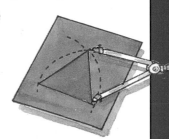

● Equilateral triangle: Draw a line and open the compass to the length of the line. Put the compass point on one end of the line and draw an arc. Put the point on the other end of the line and draw another arc. Draw a line from where the two arcs cross to each end of the line.

● Isosceles triangle: Draw a short line. Open the compass so it is longer than the line. Draw two arcs as you did above. Draw a line from where the arcs cross to each end of the line.

● Right-angled: Make a right angle measurer by folding any sized scrap of cardboard roughly in half. Fold it again so the folded edge meets itself neatly. Draw along the straight edges of your measurer then join the ends of the line with a ruler.

● Scalene: Easy! Just draw a triangle with no equal sides.

# PYRAMIDS

A tetrahedron might sound like an alien from outer space, but it's not! It is a three-dimensional shape, a pyramid with four faces. What makes a tetrahedron special is that all four faces are triangles. It is also called a triangular-based pyramid. You have probably seen other pyramid shapes, like those in Egypt. Square-based pyramids have four triangular faces and one square face.

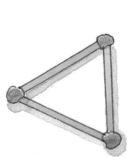

PYRAMID SKELETONS! Dare you attempt the pyramid skeleton challenge?

**1** If you feel brave enough you will need some straws, scissors, and modeling clay.

**2** Cut six straws to about 4in long.

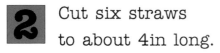

**3** Join three straws in a triangle with the modeling clay.

**4** Now stick a straw in each of the three corners and bend them over until they meet at the top. Secure them with some more modeling clay.

# HELPFUL HINTS

● You don't need to measure each straw with a ruler to get the same length. A quick way of doing it is to cut one to the length you want, then use that straw as a measure against the other straws.

**5** You have made the skeleton of a tetrahedron. Can you make the skeleton of a square-based pyramid with eight straws?

## MORE IDEAS

● Try making a star skeleton. You will need 36 straws of the same length. Don't make the straws too long otherwise the skeleton might become weak.

Make a cube from 12 of the straws.

● On each of the faces make a pyramid with four more straws. In no time you will have made a beautiful star!

# CIRCLES

Trace around a plate on some paper and cut it out. You can find the center of the **circle** by folding it in half twice. The center is where the folds meet. Draw a line along the fold that crosses the center of a circle. This line is called the **diameter**. The length of the circle's edge is called the **circumference**.

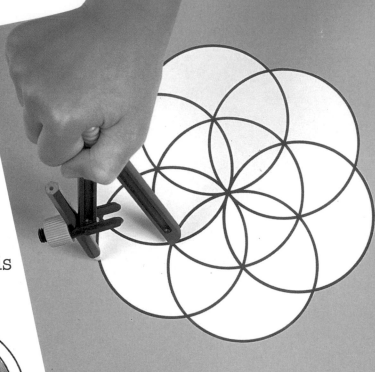

Diameter

## DRAWING DAISIES

**1** You can make beautiful flower shapes by drawing circles! All you need is a compass, paper, markers, and pencils.

**2** Draw a circle in the middle of a piece of paper. Pick up the compass but don't move the arms! Place the point anywhere on the circumference and draw another circle.

**3** Put the point of the compass on one of the places where the two circles meet and draw the third circle.

**4** Draw a fourth circle where the edge of two of the circles meet like this. Keep drawing circles until you have made a lovely pattern.

**5** Now you can decorate your flower with beautiful colors and make a fabulous display!

# HELPFUL HINTS

● You don't have to have a compass to make these patterns. It is easy to make your own circle drawer!

● You will need a piece of cardboard, scissors, a push pin, and a pencil. Cut out a strip of cardboard. Make a hole with the pin at each end of the cardboard. Leave the pin in the cardboard and push the pencil through the other hole. Now you can draw lots of circles!

## MORE IDEAS

● Try drawing different patterns. First draw a circle then place the point of the compass on the edge and draw another circle. Draw a third circle where the two meet. Now mark all the points on the edge of the shape where two circles meet and draw three more circles. Repeat this as many times as you like. Do you notice a tessellating pattern?

# STRETCHING CIRCLES

Shapes can be changed by making them bigger, smaller, and in many other ways, too. One interesting way of changing circles is to stretch them. When a circle is stretched it becomes oval or an ellipse.

MAKING FACES

**1** To make faces you need more than your own face and a mirror! Find an old photograph or a picture of a face from a magazine. Make sure the face fills as much of the picture as possible.

**2** Place a compass point at the center of the face and lightly draw as large a circle as possible. Cut out the circle.

**3** Turn it upside down and cut lines across the circle from one side of the face to the other about six or seven times like this. You could make your cuts straight or wiggly.

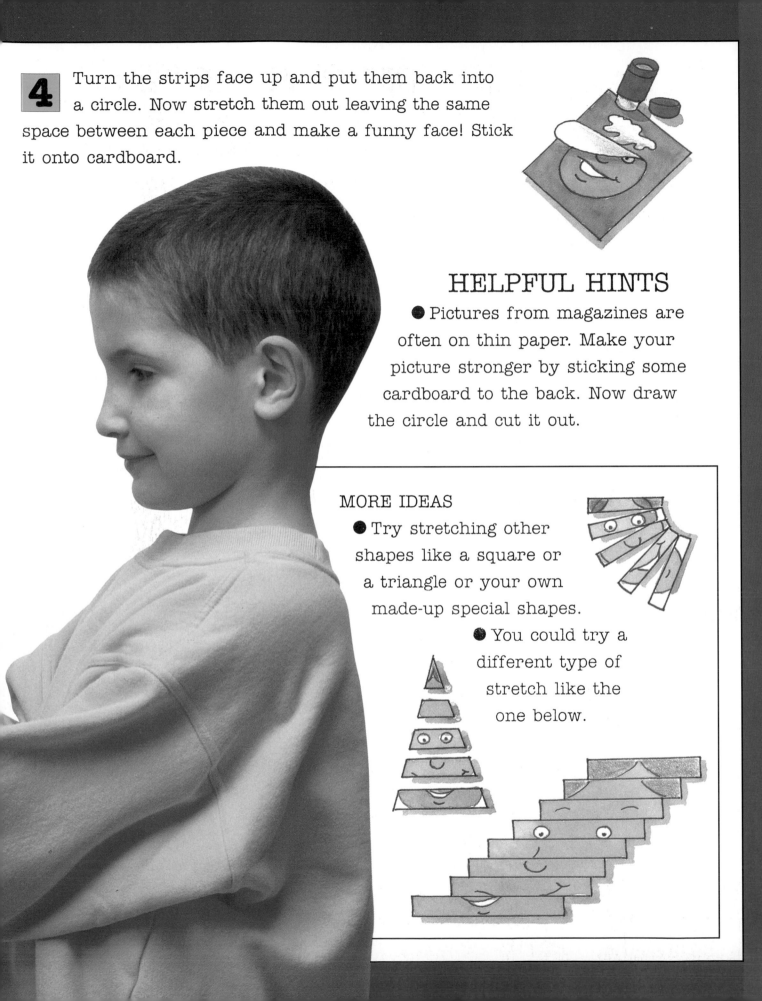

**4** Turn the strips face up and put them back into a circle. Now stretch them out leaving the same space between each piece and make a funny face! Stick it onto cardboard.

## HELPFUL HINTS

● Pictures from magazines are often on thin paper. Make your picture stronger by sticking some cardboard to the back. Now draw the circle and cut it out.

### MORE IDEAS

● Try stretching other shapes like a square or a triangle or your own made-up special shapes.

● You could try a different type of stretch like the one below.

# CENTERS, SECTORS, AND CONES

Radius

When you draw a circle with a compass, the compass point is the center of the circle. The distance between the center and the edge of a circle is called the **radius**. If you draw a line from the center to the edge of the circle it will always be the same length. If two lines are drawn it looks as though a wedge of cake has been cut. This wedge is called a sector.

## HATS

It is a lot of fun designing party hats! To make your hats you will need plenty of colored cardboard, markers, scissors, tape, a compass, streamers, and shapes to decorate your hats.

Sector

**1** Draw a large circle on some cardboard with your compass. Now draw the radius. Draw another radius. You could make the sector either wide or narrow.

**2** Cut out the circle and the sector and carefully stick the edges of the larger sector together like this. You have now made a **cone**!

# HELPFUL HINTS

● To help the hats stay on your friends' heads make a small hole on the inside of the hat on each side close to the ears. Thread some elastic through the hole. Tie a knot, to stop the elastic from slipping back through the hole, and do the same on the other side.

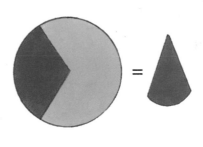

**3** Last of all, decorate your hat with shapes and streamers!

## MORE IDEAS

● Experiment by cutting out different sizes of sectors from the circles. How does it change the shape of the cone?

● Cutting out a large sector will make the hat more pointed. If you cut out a small sector the hat will stay quite flat.

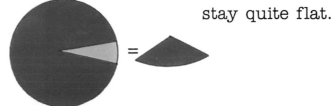

# POLYGONS

A polygon is a flat two-dimensional shape with three or more straight sides. Some have special names. A pentagon has five sides. Hexagons have six sides. Heptagons have seven sides. Octagons have eight sides.

## FEELY SHAPES

If you don't know the names of shapes, how well can you describe them?

**1** Three or more players can play Feely Shapes. You will need some cardboard, scissors, pencils, a ruler, paper, and a bag to hide the shapes you make.

**2** Draw some shapes on the cardboard. The lines must be straight but can be any length and the corners can be any angle.

Now cut them out and put them in the bag.

**3** One of the players chooses a shape inside the bag. They must keep it hidden and describe it to the other players without looking at it!

**4** The other players try and draw the shape that is being described. When the other players have finished their sketches, take the shape out of the bag.

## HELPFUL HINTS

● With some practice you can become very good at describing polygons.

● Try to describe the number of straight sides. Do they feel long or short?

● What do the corners of the shape feel like? Are they very pointed?

### MORE IDEAS

● Try playing the same game again, but this time include shapes with curved edges, like circles and ellipses, or your own made-up shape!

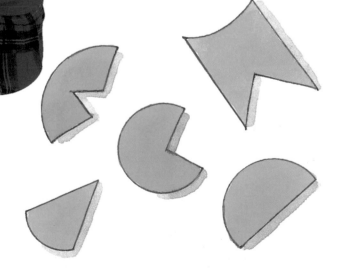

**5** The winner is the player that has made the best drawing of the polygon.

# TANGRAMS

A tangram is an ancient Chinese shape puzzle, a little like a jigsaw. Some people think tangrams are about 2,500 years old! It is made up of five triangles, a square, and a parallelogram, which is another four-sided shape.

## CATS AND DRAGONS

To make the tangram shapes you need a square of thin cardboard, markers, a ruler, and a pair of scissors.

**1** Draw a grid of 16 squares on the cardboard like this. Copy the tangram shapes from below with a marker and ruler.

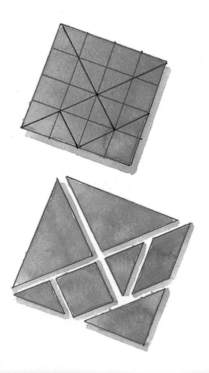

**2** Cut out the seven shapes and mix them up. Can you put them back together to make a square? Challenge your friends and see if they can make a square!

**3** Perhaps you found that easy! But can you arrange all seven shapes to make a rectangle?

**4** Try making a cat shape with the tangram pieces. Remember, you must use all seven pieces.

# HELPFUL HINTS

● You can make the grid for the tangram by folding the square piece of thin cardboard in half. Fold it in half again in the same direction. Unfold the square and repeat the folding from top to bottom. Your cardboard is now ready for you to copy the tangram shapes.

## MORE IDEAS

● Why not make up your own tangram puzzle? Each puzzle must use all seven pieces.

● First arrange your pieces carefully on some paper. Draw around the outline lightly in pencil.

● Go over the outline again using a ruler and a marker to make it clearer. Last of all, give your puzzle a name like "the dragon" and challenge a friend to match the tangram shapes to your puzzle.

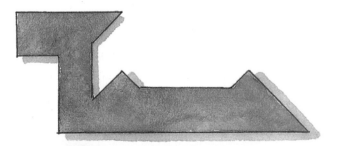

# POLYHEDRA

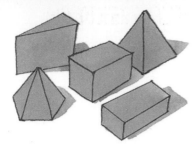

A polyhedron is a three-dimensional shape. It can have any number of faces. A tetrahedron has four triangular faces and a cube has six square faces. How many faces do you think an octahedron has? That's right, eight faces!

BUILD IT!

If you look carefully around your home, you can find lots of different shapes: a box of cereal, a cylinder from the inside of a toilet paper roll, a ball, a die, or cube. Perhaps you have some wooden building blocks.

**1** To play Build It! you need two of each shape. Collect about five pairs of identical shapes. If you want to, you could paint them all the same color, but check with an adult first.

**2** Now sit back-to-back with a friend. Build a model with all your shapes but make sure your friend can't see!

**3** Try to describe how your model is built as clearly as you can. Can your friend match your model exactly?

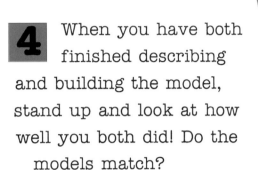

**4** When you have both finished describing and building the model, stand up and look at how well you both did! Do the models match?

## HELPFUL HINTS

● It helps to describe the position of each shape. You might say...

the cube is on top of
*or*
to the right of
*or*
underneath
*or*
next to
*or*
touching the corner of

How else can you help your partner?

### MORE IDEAS

● Collect some more three-dimensional shapes and play this fun memory game. Put all the shapes on a table and let your friends have a look. Now have your friends turn away while you remove one of the shapes. Change the position of the remaining shapes then shout "ready!" Your friends now have to try and guess which shape you have taken!

# CONTENTS

# Chapter Six

# Plotting Points and Position

# COMPASS POINTS

For years sailors and explorers have found their way by following the points on a compass. The magnetic needle always points to the north so you can work out the other directions, south, west, and east. Sometimes, other points are shown in between north, south, east, and west. Halfway between north and west is — you've guessed it, northwest!

## PIRATE'S TREASURE!

**1** This is a good party game. You must direct the pirate to the treasure! You will need a blindfold, a big box of candy for the treasure, a large sheet of paper, and markers.

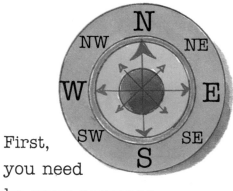

**2** First, you need to make your compass. See Helpful Hints for tips on how to do this.

**3** To play the game, let everyone take a look at the compass. Choose a pirate and an assistant to help her. Blindfold the pirate and stand her on the compass. Spin her around, but make sure she ends up facing north.

**4** Hide the treasure somewhere in the room. Then the assistant must direct the pirate to the treasure. He might give directions like, "Turn east and take two steps forward. Now turn northeast and move four steps ..." How long does it take to find the treasure?

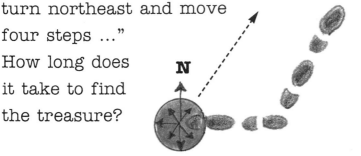

# HELPFUL HINTS

● One way to remember where the different points of the compass are is to compare them to a clock face. If north is at 12 o'clock, then east is at 3 o'clock, south is at 6 o'clock, and west is at 9 o'clock.

● Another way is to make up a phrase for the letters N, E, S, and W, the initials of the main points on the compass as you move around clockwise. **N**eptune **E**ats **S**ea **W**eed is one. Can you think of another?

● You can make your own compass by folding a piece of paper into quarters. Now fold in half again to make a triangular shape like this. Unfold the paper. Now you can draw in all the compass points and decorate it to look like a real pirate's compass!

# MAP REFERENCES

Finding somewhere on a map could be quite a problem, but luckily map makers make it easier for us. They draw a grid of criss-crossing lines over the map and in between each line is usually a letter or a number. Each part of the map can now be found by a reference or address.

## CUP CRAZY
Can you use map references to find some candy?

**1** You will need markers, a ruler, candy, cardboard, and 16 plastic cups. You could paint them so you can't see through them.

**2** Draw out a grid of 16 squares on the cardboard and place a cup upside down on each square. Label the squares A, B, C, and D along the bottom and label the numbers 1, 2, 3, and 4 up the sides.

**3** Secretly hide a piece of candy under one of the cups and ask your friend to guess where it is. They have to guess using a reference, for example, C2. You reply either "hot" if they have guessed correctly, "warm" if they are just one cup away, or "cold" if they are farther away.

**4** How quickly can you find the candy?

## HELPFUL HINTS

● It is a good habit to get used to saying the letter reference first and then the number as this is the usual way that map references are used.

A2 or C4

### MORE IDEAS

● You could play the same game but with even more cups!

● How many can you find? Make sure you ask an adult first before you borrow them for the game. They don't have to be laid out in a square — what about a rectangular grid?

● You could also play the game by hiding more than one candy; try two or three.

# COORDINATES

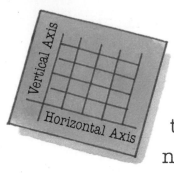

**Coordinates** are used to plot points on a graph. On a flat, two-dimensional graph a pair of numbers, for example (5,1), is used to show a position. The first number shows how far to move along the **horizontal axis** and the second number shows how far up the **vertical axis** the point is.

## CONNECTIONS

**1** Connections is a game for two players where you use coordinates to score points. You will need some cardboard, a ruler, markers, two dice, and two different sets of colored counters.

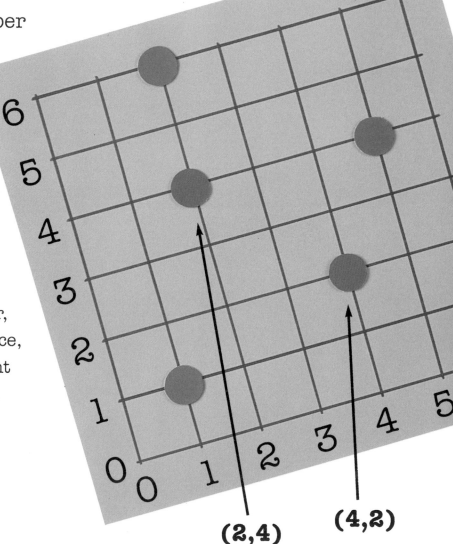

(2,4)   (4,2)

**2** Make a game board like the one above. Make all the lines about 1 inch apart. Put a 0 where the lines meet then 1-6 on each axis.

**3** The first player throws the two dice. If a 4 and a 2 are thrown, you can choose to place a counter on either (2,4) or (4,2).

**4** Now the second player must throw the dice and place their counter in an empty position.

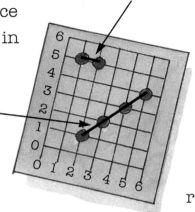

2 points

4 points

**5** Every time you can place a counter, score one point. If you make a line of two counters, score two points. A line of three scores three points and so on.

**6** Keep a record of your scores on a chart. The player with the highest score after 12 turns wins.

# HELPFUL HINTS

● If you find it difficult to remember which coordinate comes first, you might find it helpful to think of it as "along the hall," for the first number and "up the stairs" for the second!

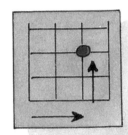

## MORE IDEAS

● X Marks the Spot is a great coordinates game. You can play with the Connections grid.

● The first player secretly decides the coordinates of their hidden point, (2,2) for example, writes it on some paper, and puts it in an envelope.

● The other player guesses where it is — let's say they guess (4,4).

● Now the first player gives a clue by saying how many straight line spaces away their secret X point is. You can't count diagonal lines. In this example it is four spaces away.

● How quickly can you find where X marks the spot?

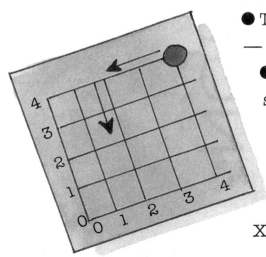

# WHICH WAY?

Have you ever been lost in a maze? Mazes are full of right and left turns, and a lot of dead ends. The secret of escape is knowing which direction to take!

## MINOTAUR MAZES

In Greek legend, a beast called the Minotaur lived in a maze. The maze was so complex no one ever escaped!

**1** You can make your own Minotaur Mazes. You will need a large piece of plain paper, play dough, paint, and pencils.

**2** Roll the play dough out into long, thin sausages. These will be the walls of your maze.

**3** Place the thin rolls on the paper with some right and left turns like this.

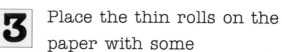

**4** Make sure you leave an entrance to the maze and an exit. How difficult can you make the maze?

**5** When you are happy with your maze, paint over the paper and play dough walls.

## HELPFUL HINTS

● When you paint over the paper and play dough don't make the mixture too wet. It can leak under the play dough so it becomes difficult to see where the walls are.

**6** Let the paint dry then remove the play dough. Draw around the edges of the walls to make them stand out clearly and challenge a friend to escape through your Minotaur Maze!

### MORE IDEAS

● The Celtic people also loved mazes. Many of their designs were curved like this one.

● Can you make a maze with curves to fit inside a circle?

# QUARTER TURNS

When people talk about turns they often mean a quarter turn to the left or a quarter turn to the right. A quarter turn is a little like the turn between the edges on the corner of a square.

WRAPPING PAPER PRINTS

This is a great way of using turns to make wrapping paper. You will need some large potatoes, paint, a ruler, a pencil, a knife (ask an adult first), and as big a sheet of paper as you can find.

**1** Cut the potato in half like this. With a dark pencil make a design on the base of the cut potato.

**2** Ask an adult to help you to use the knife to cut away the potato. Leave the design standing out.

**3** On the top of the potato make a "V" shape to show the direction of your potato printing block. Now you are ready to print!

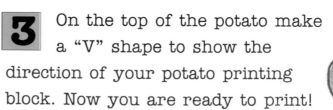

**4** Choose a color and cover your block design with paint. Start at the top left of your sheet, making sure the "V" arrow is pointing directly toward you, then gently press the potato onto the sheet.

**5** Now turn the potato a quarter turn **clockwise** like this and make another print in the next square.

## HELPFUL HINTS

● The pattern may look better if you space the prints evenly. You can make guidelines as part of the pattern by using an old ruler and a paintbrush or markers. Rest the ruler on the paper and paint or draw a line. Estimate where to put the ruler next. Be careful how you pick up the ruler, it might smear the paint on the paper!

**6** Keep repeating the pattern of turns until you cover the whole sheet.

## MORE IDEAS

● You could make the pattern more interesting by using two colors.

● Why not try using different potato block designs to create more unusual patterns.

# ROTATING TILES

People from many countries around the world love using tile patterns in their homes and on buildings. Some of the swirling patterns look very complicated, but are quite easy to make if you follow the pattern of turns carefully.

## BLOCKS

**1** You will need a block of wood about 2 inches long and 2 inches wide, scissors, a pencil, a ruler, thick string, strong glue, paint, and paper.

**2** Mark the top of the block with an arrow so you will be able to see which way it is pointing when you are making prints.

**3** On the other side make two marks on each edge of the block evenly spaced 1 inch apart.

1 in

**4** Next, cut some short lengths of string and stick them on the block. Make sure that the beginning and end of the string lead from one of the marks on the block to another.

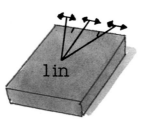

**5** Cover the string in paint and press firmly onto the paper. Pick the block up carefully, rotate it a quarter turn clockwise, and repeat the print in the next square. Keep repeating this until the grid is full.

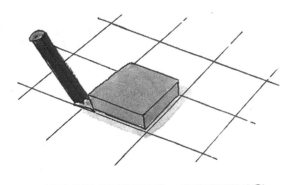

## HELPFUL HINTS

● To make your block printing as accurate as possible you might find it best to begin by drawing out the square tile pattern. Using your block, trace around the outline then move the block to the first outline and keep repeating.

### MORE IDEAS

● Make some more designs, but this time glue the string in straight lines from one mark to another like this. Sticking the string in straight and curved lines also produces some interesting effects. Try experimenting with different designs and different patterns of turns (or rotations).

# ANGLES

A quarter turn is also called a right angle. A square has four right angles and so does a rectangle. A right angle can be measured as having 90 **degrees**. Angles of less than 90 degrees are called acute. Those of more than 90 degrees are called obtuse angles.

## ANGLING

**1** Are you good at angling? To play this game you need to make 18 game cards. Draw angles on the back, make sure you draw six of each angle (acute, obtuse, and right). Why not draw a fish on the back? Helpful Hints gives advice on how to draw the angles.

**2** The object of the game is to win as many cards as possible by collecting matching angles.

**3** Shuffle the cards and lay them out flat in the "pond." The first player turns over three cards.

**4** If they are all the same type of angle, you win the cards. If they are not all the same, turn them back over, try to remember where they are, and the next player has their turn. The player with the most cards at the end wins.

# HELPFUL HINTS

● Start by making a right-angle tester. Find a scrap of cardboard and fold it in half and half again. Make sure when you make the second fold that the folded edges meet and are straight.

● Right Angles: Draw a straight line with the ruler. Sit your tester straight on the line and then mark the right angle against the side of your tester. Mark the corner with a small square.

● Acute Angles:
Make sure the angle between the two lines is less than a right angle. Rest the tester on one of the straight lines. If it covers all of the angle then the angle is acute.

● Obtuse Angles: When you use the tester you will be able to see some of the obtuse angle.

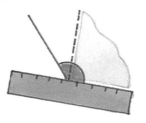

MORE IDEAS
● Half a turn is 180 degrees (see page 154). Angles greater than half a turn are called reflex angles. They look bent back on themselves! Make six reflex angles and add them to the pond.

Reflex angle

# DEGREES OF TURN

Do you remember that the angle between two lines can be measured in degrees. There are 360 degrees in one whole turn. Half a turn is 180 degrees and a quarter turn is 90 degrees.

**WHAT'S THAT ANGLE?**
How good are you at estimating angles quickly? To play this game you need to make an angle measurer.

**1** Pull the arms of a compass about 2 inches apart and draw a circle on some cardboard. Draw a smaller circle about half the size inside it then cut out the large circle.

**2** Choose a different color cardboard, make a circle with the compass arms at 1.5 inches apart, and cut that out, too.

**3** Lightly mark the center of both circles and draw a straight line from the edge to the center of the circles. Now, cut along each line.

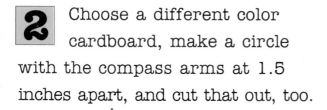

**4** Copy the degree measurement marks around the circle you have drawn on the larger circle from this example.

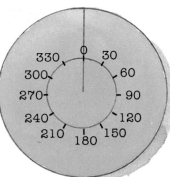

**5** Slide the two circles of cardboard into each other so they overlap and the numbers are hidden. Ask your friend to find an angle. They put their finger on the angle measurer, estimating where it is.

**6** Turn the smaller circle around to the finger and see if they have guessed correctly!

## HELPFUL HINTS

● To mark the degrees accurately on your circle follow these steps.

● After you have drawn the smaller inside circle don't move the compass arms. Draw a cross on it. Place the compass point where the cross meets the edge of the circle and make two marks on either side of the circle (**A** and **B**).

● Repeat this on the other three points where the cross meets the circle. Draw a line from each mark through the center of the circle to the other side.

# 90° MORE TURNS

If you have looked at the activities on the last few pages, you will know that the angle of turn between two lines is measured in degrees. Mathematicians usually write degrees as a little circle in the air next to the number like this, 90°.

TREASURE TROVE

**1** This is a great game for 2 or 3 players. Draw out the Treasure Trove grid onto some cardboard, using the hints on page 155 to help mark the angles accurately. Decorate it with bright colors.

**2** Now make two sets of 20 cards. For the first set you need to mark the cards 0, 1, 2, or 3. For the second set mark the cards 0 to 9.

**3** Find a treasure, like some candy, to place on each sector of the board. Now, you are ready to play!

**4** The players take turns to draw one card from the first pile and two from the second. This gives a degree measurement. If it is 248° for example, they would pick up the treasure between 240° and 270°. The player who collects the most treasure wins.

## HELPFUL HINTS

● If the first card you draw is a 0, it looks as if you have drawn a strange-looking number like 062°! You can ignore the 0, so the degree you have picked would be 62°.

## MORE IDEAS

● You could play the same sort of game, but this time design your circle like a pizza! Cut out the 12 sectors of the circle and instead of winning the treasure in the sector you take away that part of the pizza!

30°

60°

90°

20°

# MIRROR, MIRROR...

Look at your reflection in a mirror, it is exactly the same as you, except it is back to front. When a shape is reflected it might look very different or exactly the same, it depends on where you put the mirror. If it looks the same, the mirror is on a **line of symmetry.**

HALVE IT!
You might be able to draw a face, but can you draw just half?

**1** Draw a straight line down the center of a piece of paper. This is your line of symmetry where you will place a mirror after you have finished drawing.

**2** Draw half the face on just one side of the line.

**3** It might help to fold the paper in half along the line you have drawn so you don't accidentally draw on the wrong side.

**4** When you have finished your picture, put a mirror along the line of symmetry and look into it. You will see a face with two sides that are exactly the same, making a whole symmetrical face.

# HELPFUL HINTS

● Before you start to draw the face, look at your own face in a mirror. Hold a large book up across half your face like this.

How many eyes can you see? Ears? How much of your mouth can you see? What about your nose?

## MORE IDEAS

● A famous Italian inventor and artist named Leonardo da Vinci used to keep a diary. He wanted to keep his thoughts secret so he wrote it in mirror writing, back to front! It was hard to read.

● Can you write your name in mirror writing? Try it and check by holding it up to a mirror.

# REFLECTIVE SYMMETRY

Some shapes have more than one line of symmetry. This means you can put the mirror in more than one place and the shape will still look the same. A square has four lines of symmetry, a rectangle has two.

BUNTING BONANZA!

Have you ever seen bunting at a fair or a party? There are usually long lines of repeating symmetrical patterns. Often each shape in the pattern is a reflection of the one before it.

**1** It is fun making these patterns — you could make one to decorate the border of a bulletin board or frame one of your pictures.

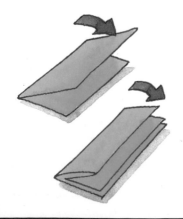

**2** Fold a piece of paper in half twice like this. If you have a long piece of paper, you can make more folds.

**3** With the paper still folded cut off a square from one end. Draw a shape in pencil on the paper — what about the outline of a person?

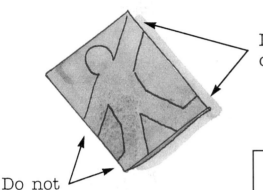

Do not cut here

Do not cut here

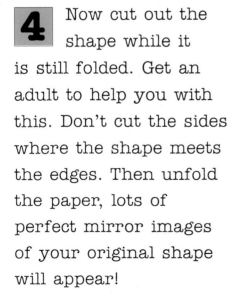

**4** Now cut out the shape while it is still folded. Get an adult to help you with this. Don't cut the sides where the shape meets the edges. Then unfold the paper, lots of perfect mirror images of your original shape will appear!

## HELPFUL HINTS

● When you draw your design, you need to make sure that it touches both sides of the square where the folds are. If you don't, when you cut out the shape all the bunting will fall into pieces!

### MORE IDEAS
● This is a great way of using reflective symmetry to make place mats for a party. Draw around a large plate and cut it out. Fold it in half and again and once more like this. Now, use the scissors to cut out small parts. When you have finished, unfold the shape and admire your handiwork!

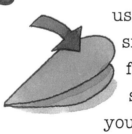

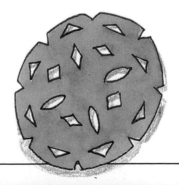

# ROTATIONAL SYMMETRY

If a shape is moved around a central point and still looks the same when it is in its new position, we say it has **rotational symmetry**. A square has rotational symmetry of order 4 because it can be rotated four times into a different position but still appears to be the same.

IN A SPIN
You can make some amazing shapes with rotational symmetry.

**1** Draw a shape on some cardboard no bigger than your hand. It might have curves or straight lines or a mixture of both. Don't make it too complicated, it might be difficult to cut out!

**2** Cut out the shape and pierce it roughly in the middle with a push pin. You might need an adult to help you with this.

**3** Put the shape in the middle of some paper and draw around it lightly. Rotate it around the push pin a quarter turn so it is facing to the right and draw around it again. Repeat this with the shape facing you then with it facing to the left.

**4** Lift the shape and the push pin off the paper and use a thick marker to draw around the edge of the new shape you have created. This new shape has rotational symmetry of order 4. You will find that it can be rotated to four different positions and still look the same.

**5** Cut out the shape, turn it over so you can't see the pencil lines, and stick it on a sheet of colored paper to make it look good.

## HELPFUL HINTS

● When you are rotating the shape on the paper, put a thick wad of newspaper underneath, otherwise the pin might make a hole in the table!

### MORE IDEAS

● It is easy to make shapes with rotational symmetry of order 8. Imagine the eight points of a compass like this.

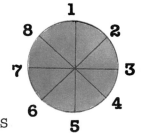

● Make a new small shape and rotate it to face each of the eight points of the compass. Draw around the edge, or perimeter, and then cut it out and mount it as you did before.

**Original shape**

# CONTENTS

# Chapter Seven

# Measuring Sizes

# LENGTH OF A LINE

How tall are you? How high can you reach? To answer questions like these we need to measure length. People used to measure length by counting up the number of hand lengths... but everyone's hands are slightly different. Now most people use a **standard measurement** like feet to measure length.

MAKE A DERBY

Can your horse be first past the winning post?

**1** Find a piece of cardboard. Fold it in half length-wise and cut it along the fold. Do the same again with another piece of cardboard and stick the four parts together to make one long strip.

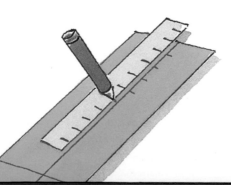

**2** Starting from the bottom of the cardboard, use a ruler with inches to draw a straight line up the middle.

**3** Mark in all the inch spaces on the line from one inch at the bottom to 12 inches, which makes one foot, at the top.

**4** Now you can decorate it to look like a race course. Make a winning post from some cardboard and stand it at one end. Cut out two cardboard shapes of horses and riders and decorate them brightly.

# HELPFUL HINTS
● To make a neat seam, turn over the cardboard. Place the strips next to each other, but not overlapping. Cover the seam with some tape. Now turn it over... a perfect finish!

**5** Cut out a rectangle of thick cardboard for each horse to stand on. To make the horse stand up, attach it to the base with two pieces of play dough.

## MORE IDEAS
● You can make the game even more fun by making some danger cards!
● If somebody throws a 1, they must pick up a card. The message might say "Horse frightened by mouse, miss a turn" or how about "High fence, go back 4in!"

**6** Place your horses at the start and take turns to roll the die and move your horse forward. The first past the post wins!

# MEASURING CURVES

The difficult thing with rulers is that they are always straight. Unfortunately, most of the world isn't. In fact, it is wonderful how wiggly and bendy the world is. Without bumps and curves the world would be a far less interesting place! So, how can you go about measuring them?

## WIGGLY WORMS

How good are your friends at guessing the right length of straight lines? What about wiggly lines? Make some wiggly worms to find out!

**1** Find some string or thick colored cord and measure out some different lengths against a ruler. You could cut lengths of 2, 4, 6, and 8 inches.

**2** Stick the lengths of string in a wiggly line on pieces of cardboard. These will be your worms. Now draw around each worm on the cards and decorate each worm to look really slimy!

**3** Write the length of each worm on the back of the cards so you don't forget.

4in 8in

**4** Challenge your friends to guess the length of each worm. The person that makes the nearest guess is the winner!

## HELPFUL HINTS

● If some of your friends find it hard to make a good guess, you could show them how to use a "rule of thumb" to help.

Strangely enough, with this "rule of thumb" you use your little finger! Most little fingers are about 0.25in wide so you can use it to move along the back of the worm to estimate its length.

### MORE IDEAS

● Why don't you try estimating the length of edges! If you have got some old vegetables, cut them in half

and draw around the edge on a piece of paper. Guess how long each edge is and write it down.

● You can find out how long the edge really is by using some string to match along the edge of the outline and mark off the length. Next, straighten the string and measure its length against a ruler and check to see how close you really were!

# VITAL STATISTICS

"You have grown so tall!" Whenever you meet someone who hasn't seen you for a while it's usually the first thing they say. Sometimes, people call measurements of the body the vital statistics. You need to know yours to find clothes that will fit and comfortable shoes.

## SKELETONS
You can make a skeleton to show your vital statistics!

**1** Find some cardboard and cut it up into long strips.

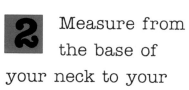

**2** Measure from the base of your neck to your hips with a tape measure. Tape some strips together to match the measurement. This will be the backbone. Write this on the strip so you don't forget.

**3** Now measure the width of your hips. Cut a strip to match and attach it to the other strip with a butterfly pin. Put the pin through both pieces of paper and bend the arms back. Ask an adult to help you with this.

**4** Measure other parts of your body and pin them all on to make your skeleton! How many parts can you include? What about your fingers and toes?

## HELPFUL HINTS

● You could draw a stick figure first to show the parts of your body you are going to measure. As you measure each part, write it down on the stick figure picture.

● You can then cut all the strips of cardboard to the right length and join them together. You could make some strips thicker to make your skeleton more realistic.

● You can add a skull to your skeleton by measuring around your head with a tape measure. Make a strip to match the length, loop it over, and stick it together.

● Do the same again, measuring around your head from top to bottom. Loop the strip around and stick it to the first skull loop.

● Make a bright face from pieces of cardboard and stick this onto the head with tape.

# AREA

Have you ever had new tiles put into your bathroom or kitchen? We call the space you want to cover, the **area**. Often the tiles are square shaped and this is how the size of an area is measured — in squares.

## TILE FLIPPING

To win this game you need to capture the area covered by the tiles by flipping all the squares over to your color.

**1** Find two pieces of different colored cardboard the same size. Stick them together back to back. Draw a square grid on the cardboard with lines about 1in apart. The squares will be your tiles.

**2** Cut out 16 tiles. Now you are ready to play the game.

**3** Turn the tiles so that eight are showing red and eight are green. Arrange them in a square.

**4** The first player is the green team. He rolls a die. If a 3 is rolled, then three cards are turned over from red to green.

**5** Now it is the red player's turn. He has one throw and turns back the number of cards shown on the die from green to red.

**6** The die is then passed back and the battle to win all sixteen squares continues until one of the players captures them all!

## MORE IDEAS
● To play Tile Flipping you arranged the 16 square tiles to make a bigger square shape. What other numbers of tiles can you find that can be arranged to make a square? You could try four tiles, but there are others, too. These are special numbers that are called square numbers!

# MEASURING AREA

Like measuring length, not everything in the world comes in straight lines or simple squares that are easy to count and measure. Most areas that need measuring come in all sorts of unusual shapes.

BIG FOOT?
What do you think covers the greatest area, your foot or your hand? Take a quick look at them and press one against the other.

**1** Draw a grid of squares on a piece of paper with your ruler. Helpful Hints tells you how to do this if you are stuck.

**2** Place one of your feet on the grid and get a friend to draw around it with a bright marker. Color in the shape of the foot so you can see it clearly.

**3** Do the same again on another grid with your hand.

**4** To find the area of the foot, count all the whole squares inside the print.

but not one like this.

**5** Next, count all the squares that are more than half covered by the print. You would count a square like this...

**6** What is the total area covered by your foot? Now count the squares covered by your hand. Which is the largest?

## HELPFUL HINTS

● To make the grid of squares, line your ruler up with the edge of the paper and draw a straight line. Move the ruler along the paper so that the edge is now resting on the line you have just drawn. Draw a new line and repeat this across the page. Do the same moving across the page in the other direction like this to make the squares.

### MORE IDEAS
● Why don't you find out the area covered by your mom or dad's foot?

● Make a guess and then find out. But watch out, they may have smelly feet!

# CALCULATING AREA

You can't always find the area of something by counting squares! Sometimes, it is easier to calculate area by using multiplication tables. If you need to find the area of a rectangle all you need to do is multiply the length by the width. So, for a rectangle that has sides of 2in and 4in the area is 2in x 4in = 8 **square inches**!

## AREA ARITHMETIC

To be good at this game your friends will need good estimation skills and a good memory for number facts.

**1** Plan some rectangles to draw on a piece of scrap paper.

5in

2in

**2** The first one might be 2in long and 5in wide, so the area would be 2in x 5in = 10 square inches.

4in

4in

**3** The second might be 4in long and 4in wide, so the area would be 4in x 4in = 16 square inches. It is easy to see if you mark off the squares.

**4** Make about ten different rectangles and draw them on cardboard. Don't mark in the individual squares. Mark each rectangle with a letter. Write the answers on a piece of paper and hide it from your friend.

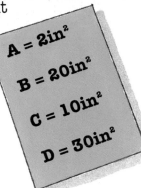

A = 2in²
B = 20in²
C = 10in²
D = 30in²

## HELPFUL HINTS

● To make it easier for some of your friends to play, you could draw a square inch on the corner of each card to help them with their estimates.

**1 square inch** ──▶

**5** Now, challenge your friends to estimate the area of each of the rectangles. The person who estimates most accurately wins!

### MORE IDEAS

● Have you noticed that some rectangles look different but have the same area?

● A rectangle with sides of 3in and 6in and one with sides 9in and 2in long both have the same area because 3in x 6in = 18 square inches and 2in x 9in = 18 square inches.

● Make up a new quiz. This time make all the rectangles different shapes but the same area. Do you think your friends will notice your trick?

# PERIMETER

The perimeter of a shape is the line that goes around its edge. It is quite easy to figure out the perimeter of some shapes with straight edges. You can measure the length of each edge with a ruler then add up the lengths to find the total. The lengths of each side of this triangle are 3in, 4in, and 5in. The total length is 3in + 4in + 5in = 12in.

## STRING SHAPES

This is a fun way of making lots of strange and unusual shapes that all have the same perimeter length.

**1** Measure out a piece of string about three feet long. Join the ends of the string with a piece of tape like this.

**2** Find a large piece of paper and put the string on it. Now, arrange the string to make an interesting shape. Make sure the string doesn't loop over itself.

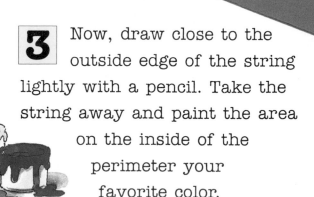

**3** Now, draw close to the outside edge of the string lightly with a pencil. Take the string away and paint the area on the inside of the perimeter your favorite color.

**4** Now, paint the outside a different color. Wait until the paint dries and then go over the perimeter again with a thick black marker to make it stand out.

**5** Try making a new shape with the same piece of string — something that looks completely different. The perimeter will still be the same!

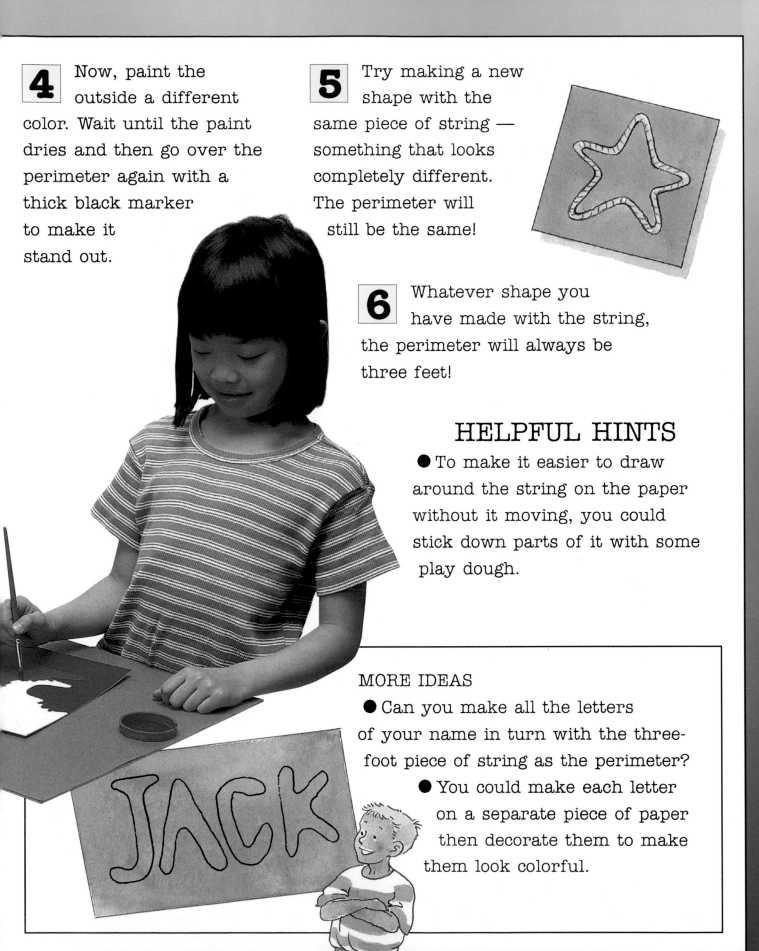

**6** Whatever shape you have made with the string, the perimeter will always be three feet!

## HELPFUL HINTS
● To make it easier to draw around the string on the paper without it moving, you could stick down parts of it with some play dough.

### MORE IDEAS
● Can you make all the letters of your name in turn with the three-foot piece of string as the perimeter?
● You could make each letter on a separate piece of paper then decorate them to make them look colorful.

# AREA AND PERIMETER

The perimeter goes all the way around a shape. The inside of the shape is called the area. Some shapes have the same area but the length of the perimeter may be longer or shorter, it doesn't always stay the same.

## SQUARE SHUFFLING

Can you shuffle eight squares to make the longest possible perimeter?

**1** When you have made eight square cards try an arrangement. One side of each square must touch one side of at least one other square.

**2** If you arranged the cards like this, the perimeter would be 14 sides long.

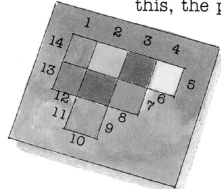

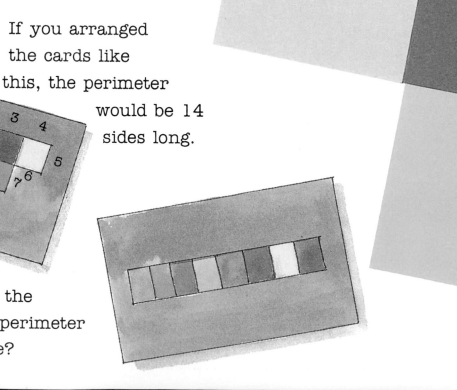

**3** What is the longest perimeter you can make?

**4** If you think you have found the longest perimeter try to find the shortest!

## HELPFUL HINTS

● A quick way of making a square from a piece of cardboard is to gently fold over one of the corners to touch the side edge and then make a mark where it meets. Then fold over the end to that mark and make a sharp crease like this. Cut along the crease and you have a square.

Cut along crease

### MORE IDEAS

● You can make the longest perimeter in lots of different ways. Here is one way of doing it.

● Did you find any others? Can you see how arrangements of squares that give the longest perimeter are similar? They all spread out the squares so that as many edges as possible of each square are part of the perimeter.

● Now you know this rule, can you quickly find a shape with twelve squares with the longest perimeter possible? It should have a perimeter 26 sides long. What would be the longest perimeter you could make if you used 24 squares?

# TO THE MAX

One problem mathematicians often face is how to get the maximum out of something. Knowing how to find the maximum amount of area when the perimeter has to stay the same is very useful for solving lots of practical problems.

THE FARMER'S FENCE
Can you help the farmer to fix his fences so that he can make as much space for his chickens as possible?

**1** The farmer is poor and can only afford 16 panels of fencing. The fences will only join together in a straight line or at right angles.

**2** The farmer decides to make a plan. You could use old burned matches, **but make sure you ask an adult first.**

**3** He started by laying out the fences like this. The area inside the perimeter of the fence is ten squares.

He tries again. This time the area is worse! Only nine squares.

**4** Can you find a better way of arranging the perimeter fencing to make the greatest possible area for the farmer's chickens?

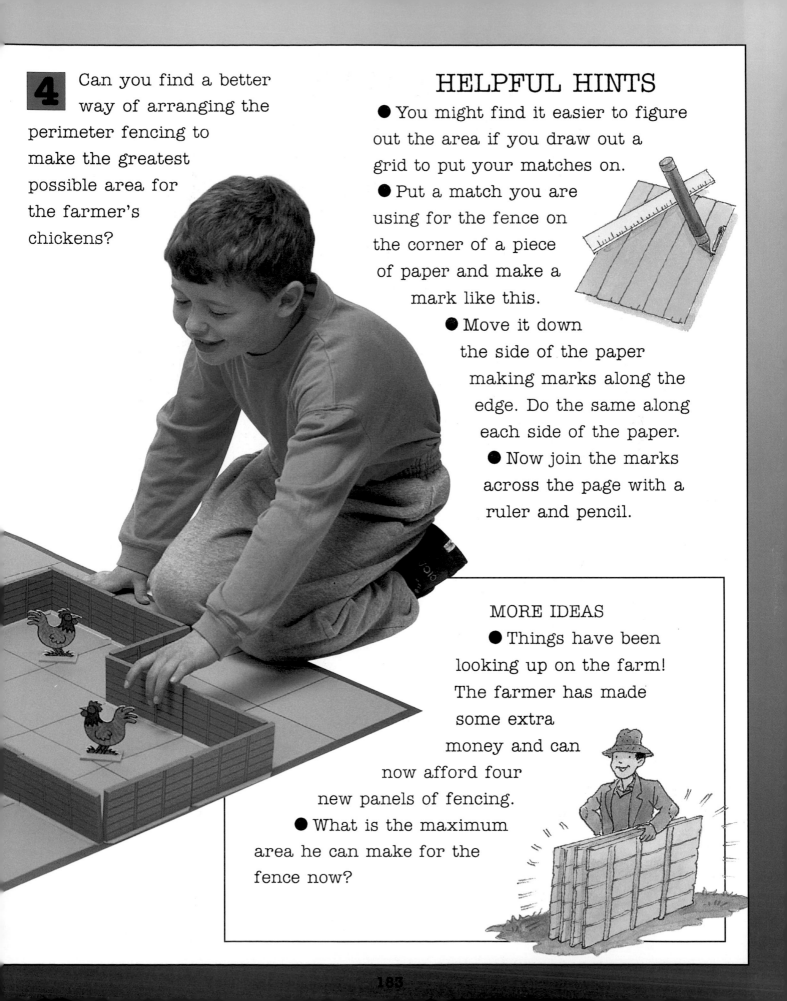

# HELPFUL HINTS

● You might find it easier to figure out the area if you draw out a grid to put your matches on.

● Put a match you are using for the fence on the corner of a piece of paper and make a mark like this.

● Move it down the side of the paper making marks along the edge. Do the same along each side of the paper.

● Now join the marks across the page with a ruler and pencil.

## MORE IDEAS

● Things have been looking up on the farm! The farmer has made some extra money and can now afford four new panels of fencing.

● What is the maximum area he can make for the fence now?

# VOLUME

You might have heard your mom or dad suggest that you "turn the volume down and play quietly!" When mathematicians use the word **volume** they are not talking about the amount of sound that is made. The volume of a shape is the amount of space it takes up. It is often measured in **cubed inches**.

MAKIN' AND SHAPIN'
Can you shape a cube of play dough into amazing monsters?

1in

**1** First of all, try making one cubed inch. Draw a square inch on a piece of paper as above.

**2** Roll some play dough into a ball. Use two rulers to squash the sides until it fits the square. Keep doing this to all the sides until you have made a cube. You might have to add more dough or take some away to make each side of the cube fit the square.

**3** Now you have made a cubed inch it doesn't matter what you do to it, squash it, pinch it or push a hole through it — it will always be one cubed inch.

**4** But one cubed inch is a little small. Draw out a square 5in by 5in. This makes an area of 5in x 5in = 25 square inches.

**5** When you have made this larger cube it will be 5in x 5in x 5in = 125 cubed inches. You can make some amazing monsters with a volume of this size!

## MORE IDEAS

● It is amazing how large the volume of some small shapes can be.

● To find the volume of a cube you have to multiply the length of the edge by itself and then once more. So, the volume of a cube that has edges 2in long would be 2in x 2in x 2in = 8 cubed inches. What is the volume of a cube with edges of 10in? What about 99in? You may need a calculator to figure out this one.

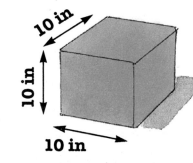

10 in
10 in
10 in
10 in

# CAPACITY

A ten-gallon hat was meant to have the **capacity** to hold ten gallons of water! Capacity is the way we measure the amount of substance a container will hold.

FILL IT UP!
How good are you at estimating the amount of water you need to fill up different containers?

**1** Ask an adult if you can borrow some different empty containers like bottles and cups from the kitchen. Now find an old bottle top and get a large jug of water.

**2** How many full bottle tops of water do you think it will take to fill up the cup for example?

**3** Write down all the different containers on a score card and make an estimate of the number of full bottle tops you think each one will hold.

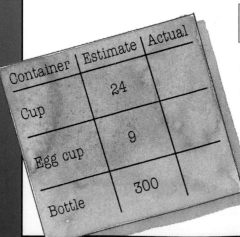

| Container | Estimate | Actual |
|-----------|----------|--------|
| Cup | 24 | |
| Egg cup | 9 | |
| Bottle | 300 | |

**4** Now try filling the cup carefully. How many can it take before the water spills over the top? Write the total down on the scorecard. The person who makes the best estimate is the winner.

## HELPFUL HINTS

● This can be quite a wet and messy game! It is a good idea to do the filling or pouring over a sink. If it is easier on a table put a towel down and place the containers on it to save everyone from getting soaked!

### MORE IDEAS

● Ask an adult if you can borrow a measuring jug from the kitchen.

● You can play a similar game with cups. Fill a cup up to the brim and tip all the water into the jug. If you look on the side of the jug, you can see the measuring marks. These might be in fluid ounces, marked fl.oz., pints, marked pt., or gallons, marked gal. See if you can estimate how far up the measuring jug the water from a different size cup will go when you pour it in. How accurate can you make your estimates?

# VOLUME OR CAPACITY?

Volume and capacity are similar. Volume is the amount of space occupied by an object and capacity refers to the amount of substance a container can hold. The capacity of a bottle holding 16 fl.oz does not change, but if you gulp some of the drink the volume of liquid is less.

WATER MUSIC
Some musical instruments make use of different volumes of air to make different notes. You can make your own bottle orchestra.

**1** Ask an adult if you can borrow a glass bottle and a measuring jug. Tap the bottle with a pencil and listen to the sound it makes.

**2** Try pouring in different volumes of water. Perhaps 8 fl.oz first.

**3** Tap the outside of the bottle with a pencil. How has the sound changed? Yes! it is a higher note. Try 16 fl.oz., then 24 fl.oz. How is the sound affected now?

**4** Try gathering some other glass bottles and make each have a different note. Can you make up a tune?

## HELPFUL HINTS

● It is easier if you use bottles that are exactly the same. When you have found the amount of water in the bottle that gives you the note you want you can keep a record of what you have done by tipping all the water back into the measuring jug and writing down the amount.

● Take a look at the number of fluid ounces you used and write it down, so when you play your composition for bottles and orchestra you will know exactly how much to pour into each container!

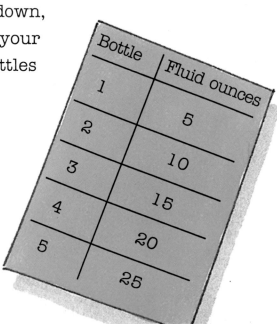

| Bottle | Fluid ounces |
|--------|--------------|
| 1 | 5 |
| 2 | 10 |
| 3 | 15 |
| 4 | 20 |
| 5 | 25 |

# CONTENTS

# Chapter Eight

# Measuring Weight and Time

# WEIGHT

How heavy is an elephant?
How about a mouse?
How heavy is the lump
of cheese in your refrigerator? We can
measure how heavy things are by weighing
them. Sometimes, the weight of an object
is called its **mass**, and we can
measure it in ounces (oz) or
pounds (lbs).

SLIMMING SNAKES
Did you know the weight
of an object never changes,
no matter what shape it is?
Make these snakes and find
out for yourself.

**2** Roll the play
dough with your
hands to make a short,
fat snake.

**1** Choose your favorite
play dough color.
Measure 5 ounces on
a **scale** and roll the play
dough into a ball.

**3** Put it back on a scale
and weigh it again. How
much does it weigh now? Yes!
Exactly the same... 5 ounces.

**4** Keep rolling out the snake. How thin can you make it?

**5** Every so often, weigh it again on the scale. It always weighs the same!

## HELPFUL HINTS

● Remember that you must not let any part of your snake break off, otherwise the weight will change. This is quite tricky when the snake gets very skinny!

### MORE IDEAS

● Weigh out another 5oz of play dough and make another animal, perhaps a dog. Although it looks very different from the snake, they both weigh exactly the same.

● Now make the body of an elephant with your new piece of play dough. Measure out another 3oz of dough of a different color or colors. Use this for the legs, ears, tail, and trunk. What do you think the elephant will weigh? That's right, it will weigh 8 ounces because 5oz + 3oz = 8ozs.

**6** It doesn't matter how fat or thin you make the snake, the weight never changes.

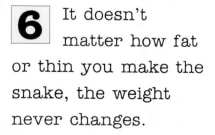

# POUNDS

Most heavy things in the house, like your mom or dad, are weighed in pounds. Can you find out how many pounds they weigh? How many pounds do you weigh?

## HOW MANY?

You can play this guessing game with your friends. Do you know how many ounces make one pound? It's sixteen! This can be written in figures like this...

**16 oz = 1 lb**

**1** First, decide what you are going to weigh. You need to estimate how many of each item it will take to make 1 pound. Make scorecards for each of your friends and write down your estimates.

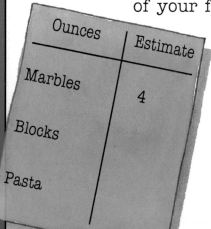

| Ounces | Estimate |
|---|---|
| Marbles | 4 |
| Blocks | |
| Pasta | |

**2** Now collect the objects to weigh and the scale you are going to measure with.

**3** If you are estimating the number of marbles needed to make 1 pound, then take turns with your friends to keep adding one more marble at a time... and watch the weight slowly rise!

**4** When the scale shows 1lb, stop and count the number of marbles on the scale. The player that made the best guess is the winner!

## HELPFUL HINTS

● If you are measuring with a bathroom scale, you will need a lightweight container to hold the things you are weighing.

● To be good at this game, it helps to get a feeling for a pound. Take a look in your kitchen cabinet. Sugar, rice, and other foods are often sold in weights of 1lb. Make sure you ask an adult before you start looking!

### MORE IDEAS

● Now that you are good at estimating the numbers of different things that make 1lb, you can play Combo Crazy! Choose any two of the objects you have been weighing. Can you combine some pasta and marbles to make 1lb? How close can you get to a pound?

# OUNCES

Which is heavier: an ounce of feathers or an ounce of nails? They are both the same! The feathers take up more space, but they weigh the same. If something is large, it doesn't mean that it is always heavier than something small. If you remember this, it will help you to play human scale.

## HUMAN SCALE

**1** Choose about ten things from around the house. What about a cushion, a cup, a book... perhaps you can think of some other interesting items. Write the name of each object on a piece of paper.

**2** Now you need to be a human scale! Which do you think is the heaviest object? Put it on the right-hand side of the table.

**3** Which do you think is the lightest? Place that on the left. Can you put everything else in order, from lightest to heaviest?

**4** Now you can find out how good you are as a human scale! Start with what you think is the lightest object and weigh it on a scale. How many ounces does it weigh?

**5** Write the weight on a card and put it next to the card of the object.

**6** Do the same for all the other objects. How good were you at getting everything in order?

## HELPFUL HINTS

● There are lots of different scales you could use. Some are easier to understand than others. You could ask an adult to help.

● If you use a kitchen scale, you can choose light and heavy objects. When using a bathroom scale, choose heavier objects only.

### MORE IDEAS

● You can play another game like this with old containers. Measure 2oz, 3oz, 4oz, 5oz, 6oz, and 8oz of rice into six containers. Cover each with a paper napkin that can be held in place with a rubber band. Mark each with a letter so you know which is which. Write down the answers on a piece of paper and hide it. Then challenge your friends to get them in the correct order from heaviest to lightest.

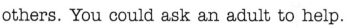

# TIME

Who is the fastest? How long does it take to travel into town? Since the beginning of time people have been trying to measure time! In the past people used other ways of measuring time. They looked at shadows made by the sun on sun dials, and at night they watched the speed at which candles melted to measure time.

DRIP, DROP, TICK, TOCK
One way you can measure time is by using a water clock. You can make your own water clock to measure exactly one minute.

**1** Find a large glass jar and stick a white strip of paper to the side like this.

**2** Find an old dishwashing liquid bottle with a cap, and carefully cut off the bottom half. You will need an adult to help you with this.

**3** Make sure you have a clock with a second hand ready.

**4** Put some play dough at the neck of the bottle. Make a small hole in it. Make sure the cap is screwed on tightly. Fill the bottle with water from the bottom.

**5** Hold it over the jar. When you are ready, take off the cap so the water starts to trickle into the jar. After one minute, mark on the paper the level the water has reached in the jar.

**6** If the water is still running through after two minutes, make another mark. When it has finished, you have made a water clock that you can fill with water and use as a timer.

MORE IDEAS
● You can play dress-up races using your water clock as a timer!
● See if you can find an old hat, shirt, pants, and some of your mom or dad's shoes. Can you or your friends put them on before the water trickles through up to the minute mark?

# MEASURING TIME

How many different watches or clocks are there in your house? What do they have in common? Clocks usually have a short hour hand and a long minute hand. Some may have a second hand, too. We measure time in seconds, minutes, and hours.

## TIME FLIES

You can play this game with a friend. The object is to start your clock at 6 o'clock and be the first to reach 9 o'clock.

**1** To make your clock, draw around a large plate on some cardboard and cut it out. Copy the hours from this example onto your circle.

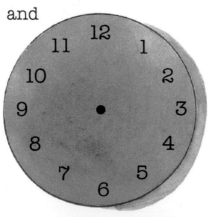

**2** To make the hands, cut out two strips of cardboard. Make one longer than the other. Use a paper fastener to push through the hands and the center of the clock face. Set the hands to 6 o'clock.

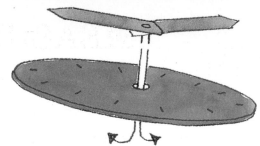

**3** Think up activities that take 5, 10, 20, or 30 minutes. Make 25 cards and write the different activities and times on them.

5 mins. brush teeth

10 mins. take a bath

20 mins. walk the dog

30 mins. do homework

**4** Take turns to take a card from the pile. Move your clock hands around the amount of minutes shown on the card. The first to reach 9 o'clock wins the game.

# JUST A MINUTE

"Just a minute..." "Wait a minute." People use sayings like these all the time, but why does a minute never seem the same length as the minute you are thinking of?

A minute is the same as sixty seconds — that's easy to remember! But it doesn't always help us to feel how long a minute is!

**TIME UP**

This is a good game to help you feel how long a minute is. You can play the game with two or more friends. You will need a watch with a second hand.

**1** The player in charge of the watch says "Go!" The other players have to guess when they think a minute is over.

TICK TICK TOCK TOCK

**2** When you think a minute has passed, you must raise your hand high in the air.

**3** When the minute is over, the person with the watch shouts "Time is over." The people who have not already raised their hands are out.

**4** The winner is the last person to raise a hand before the minute is over.

## HELPFUL HINTS

● The second hand on a clock is the one that moves the quickest. When the hand has moved around a full circle, one minute has passed.

● Sometimes, it is easiest to start timing the minute when the second hand reaches the 12, and then stop when it comes around to the 12 again.

● It may be hard to count out a minute in your head. It can help if you add a long word, like "elephant," in between each number you count. If you count "one elephant, two elephant, three elephant" this might help you to count seconds more accurately.

# WHAT DID YOU DO TODAY?

Why do parents always want to know what you've been doing at school? Don't they know that after a hard day all you want to do is play! Some people keep a note of the activities they do each day in a book called a diary.

## ACTIVITY WALLCHART

You could chart what you do each day in a diary and turn it into a colorful wallchart. You will need some cardboard, paper, scissors, pens, and a ruler.

| | | |
|---|---|---|
| 7am | 4pm | 1am |
| 8am | 5pm | 2am |
| 9am | 6pm | 3am |
| 10am | 7pm | 4am |
| 11am | 8pm | 5am |
| 12 noon | 9pm | 6am |
| 1pm | 10pm | |
| 2pm | 11pm | |
| 3pm | 12 midnight | |

**1** Draw out a diary like the one above to show each of the 24 hours in one day.

**2** As you go through your day, fill out your diary with the activities you do during each hour.

**3** Make about 35 small cards and choose some activities. Then write the activities on the cards. You might want to write "sleep" on ten of them, "watch t.v." on five, "play" on five, "meal" on five, and "school" on ten. Can you think of any others?

WATCH T.V.

SLEEP

PLAY

SCHOOL

MEAL

11am    12noon    1pm

LAY    SCHOOL    MEAL

5pm    6pm

12am

**4** Find a large piece of cardboard for your wallchart and draw on it 24 smaller squares — one square for each hour of your diary. Label each square with the hour time. Stick the chart onto your wall. Check with an adult first.

**5** Now go through your diary and for each hour stick the correct activity card onto your wallchart.

**6** When you have finished your 24 hours, you can see how much time you spent sleeping that day. How much time did you spend at school? How about playing?

# DIGITAL CLOCKS

Some clocks and watches don't have a face and hands. The time is shown in numbers, or **digits**. Usually the first two digits show the hour, and the last two the minutes. These are called digital clocks.

STOP THE CLOCK

**1** Can you arrange some matchsticks to make a time as close to the deadline as possible? Ask an adult before you use the matchsticks.

06.00

**2** You could draw a guide for your matchsticks like this.

**3** You could begin by just trying to make some different times with your matchsticks. This is how you can make eleven minutes before eight, or 07:49.

17

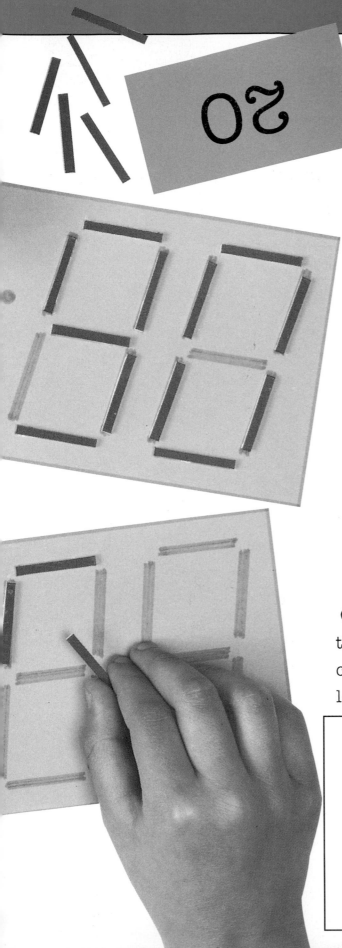

**4** Make one pile of cards and write numbers on them from 17 to 21.

**5** Make another pile of cards and write some times on them, for example 06.00.

**6** You and a friend must each pick a card from the first pile. This will show you how many sticks you can use to make the time.

**7** Now choose one time card. You must both try to arrange your sticks as near to this time as possible. The person nearest wins.

## HELPFUL HINTS

● If you find it hard to remember what the digits on a clock look like, then use a calculator to remind you — the numbers look the same.

MORE IDEAS
● You could even use the 24-hour clock. A time like one o'clock in the afternoon is shown as `13:00` hours and ten o'clock at night is `22:00` hours.

# SECONDS, MINUTES, HOURS...

How long does it take you to get to school? One minute, 15 minutes? You might say it took 900 seconds, but that would seem a little strange! There are many different measurements of time.

When we describe how long something takes, we try to use a measurement that others find easy to understand and that isn't overly exact.

HOW OLD ARE YOU?
No! not years old. That's too easy. How many hours old are you? There is a way that you can find out. You will need a calculator to help you.

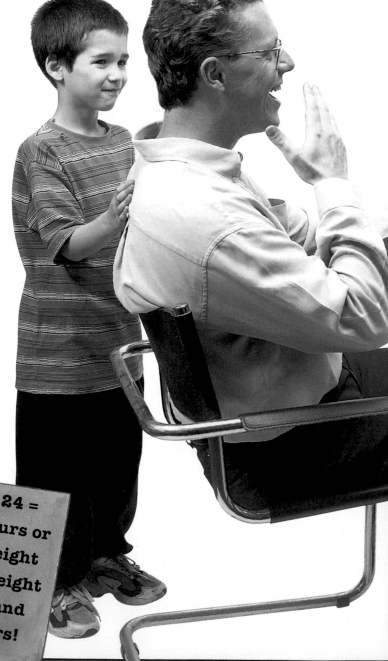

**9 x 365 = 3,285 days**

**1** Multiply your age by the number of days in a year. If you are 9 it would look like this.

**3,285 x 24 = 78,840 hours or Seventy-eight thousand, eight hundred and forty hours!**

**2** Now multiply the answer 3,285, by the number of hours in a day.

**3** Make a birthday card for your mom, dad, brother, or sister, with their age in hours on the front. Find out how many years old they will be next birthday.

35 years old
in hours
───────
35 years x
365 days x
24 hours =
───────
306,600 hours

**4** Then all you have to do is follow the same calculation. Multiply the number of years by 365, and then the answer to that by 24.

HAPPY
BIRTHDAY
**DAD**
YOU ARE
**306,600**
HOURS
OLD TODAY

**5** Thank goodness you are only making a card and not a cake for their birthday with all those candles!

MORE IDEAS
● If you want to sound very clever, you can estimate the number of minutes old someone is. A quick way to do this, is to halve the person's age and add a million on the end! So, if your friend is 10 years old, then a good estimate is that they are 5 million minutes old.

8 years old
in minutes is
8 ÷ 2 = 4
add six zeros =
───────
4,000,000
minutes old

# TIMES TABLES

| | | | |
|---|---|---|---|
| 1x1=1 | 1x4=4 | 1x7=7 | 1x10=10 |
| 2x1=2 | 2x4=8 | 2x7=14 | 2x10=20 |
| 3x1=3 | 3x4=12 | 3x7=21 | 3x10=30 |
| 4x1=4 | 4x4=16 | 4x7=28 | 4x10=40 |
| 5x1=5 | 5x4=20 | 5x7=35 | 5x10=50 |
| 6x1=6 | 6x4=24 | 6x7=42 | 6x10=60 |
| 7x1=7 | 7x4=28 | 7x7=49 | 7x10=70 |
| 8x1=8 | 8x4=32 | 8x7=56 | 8x10=80 |
| 9x1=9 | 9x4=36 | 9x7=63 | 9x10=90 |
| 10x1=10 | 10x4=40 | 10x7=70 | 10x10=100 |
| 11x1=11 | 11x4=44 | 11x7=77 | 11x10=110 |
| 12x1=12 | 12x4=48 | 12x7=84 | 12x10=120 |
| | | | |
| 1x2=2 | 1x5=5 | 1x8=8 | 1x11=11 |
| 2x2=4 | 2x5=10 | 2x8=16 | 2x11=22 |
| 3x2=6 | 3x5=15 | 3x8=24 | 3x11=33 |
| 4x2=8 | 4x5=20 | 4x8=32 | 4x11=44 |
| 5x2=10 | 5x5=25 | 5x8=40 | 5x11=55 |
| 6x2=12 | 6x5=30 | 6x8=48 | 6x11=66 |
| 7x2=14 | 7x5=35 | 7x8=56 | 7x11=77 |
| 8x2=16 | 8x5=40 | 8x8=64 | 8x11=88 |
| 9x2=18 | 9x5=45 | 9x8=72 | 9x11=99 |
| 10x2=20 | 10x5=50 | 10x8=80 | 10x11=110 |
| 11x2=22 | 11x5=55 | 11x8=88 | 11x11=121 |
| 12x2=24 | 12x5=60 | 12x8=96 | 12x11=132 |
| | | | |
| 1x3=3 | 1x6=6 | 1x9=9 | 1x12=12 |
| 2x3=6 | 2x6=12 | 2x9=18 | 2x12=24 |
| 3x3=9 | 3x6=18 | 3x9=27 | 3x12=36 |
| 4x3=12 | 4x6=24 | 4x9=36 | 4x12=48 |
| 5x3=15 | 5x6=30 | 5x9=45 | 5x12=60 |
| 6x3=18 | 6x6=36 | 6x9=54 | 6x12=72 |
| 7x3=21 | 7x6=42 | 7x9=63 | 7x12=84 |
| 8x3=24 | 8x6=48 | 8x9=72 | 8x12=96 |
| 9x3=27 | 9x6=54 | 9x9=81 | 9x12=108 |
| 10x3=30 | 10x6=60 | 10x9=90 | 10x12=120 |
| 11x3=33 | 11x6=66 | 11x9=99 | 11x12=132 |
| 12x3=36 | 12x6=72 | 12x9=108 | 12x12=144 |

# FRACTION WALL

| ⅑ | ⅑ | ⅑ | ⅑ | ⅑ | ⅑ | ⅑ | ⅑ | ⅑ |
|---|---|---|---|---|---|---|---|---|

| ⅛ | ⅛ | ⅛ | ⅛ | ⅛ | ⅛ | ⅛ | ⅛ |
|---|---|---|---|---|---|---|---|

| ⅐ | ⅐ | ⅐ | ⅐ | ⅐ | ⅐ | ⅐ |
|---|---|---|---|---|---|---|

| ⅙ | ⅙ | ⅙ | ⅙ | ⅙ | ⅙ |
|---|---|---|---|---|---|

| ⅕ | ⅕ | ⅕ | ⅕ | ⅕ |
|---|---|---|---|---|

| ¼ | ¼ | ¼ | ¼ |
|---|---|---|---|

| ⅓ | ⅓ | ⅓ |
|---|---|---|

| ½ | ½ |
|---|---|

| 1 |
|---|

# COMMON PATTERNS

## Triangular Numbers

1 = ●

3 = ●
    ● ●

6 = ●
    ● ●
    ● ● ●

10 = ●
     ● ●
     ● ● ●
     ● ● ● ●

15 = ●
     ● ●
     ● ● ●
     ● ● ● ●
     ● ● ● ● ●

## Square Numbers

1 = ●
(1x1)

4 = ● ●
(2x2) ● ●

9 = ● ● ●
(3x3) ● ● ●
      ● ● ●

16 = ● ● ● ●
(4x4) ● ● ● ●
      ● ● ● ●
      ● ● ● ●

To find out the next triangular number, add another row to the bottom of the triangle. Each row has one more dot.

## Cubed Numbers

1 cubed = 1 (1x1x1)

2 cubed = 8 (2x2x2)

3 cubed = 27 (3x3x3)

4 cubed = 64 (4x4x4)

**3 cubed =**

# COMMON GRAPHS

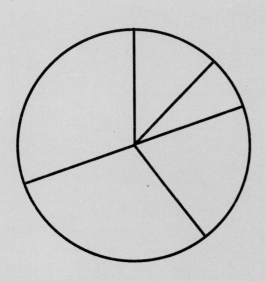

**Pie Chart**

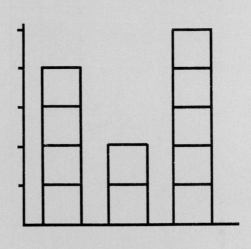

**Bar Graph**

**Pictogram**

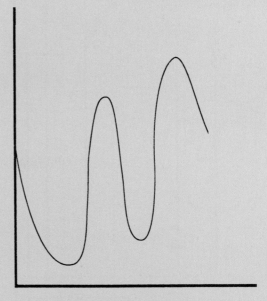

**Line Graph**

# COMMON
# SHAPES

## 2D SHAPES

**Triangle** →

**Pentagon** ←

**Hexagon** →

**Octagon** ←

**Parallelogram** →

## 3D SHAPES

**Cube** →

**Cuboid** ←

**Cone** →

**Cylinder** ←

**Tetrahedron** →

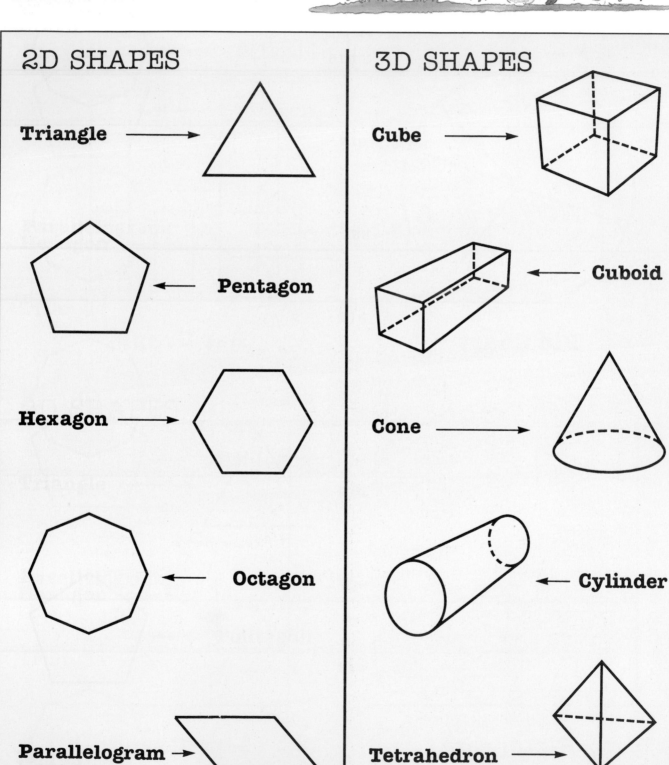

# ANGLES AND COMPASSES

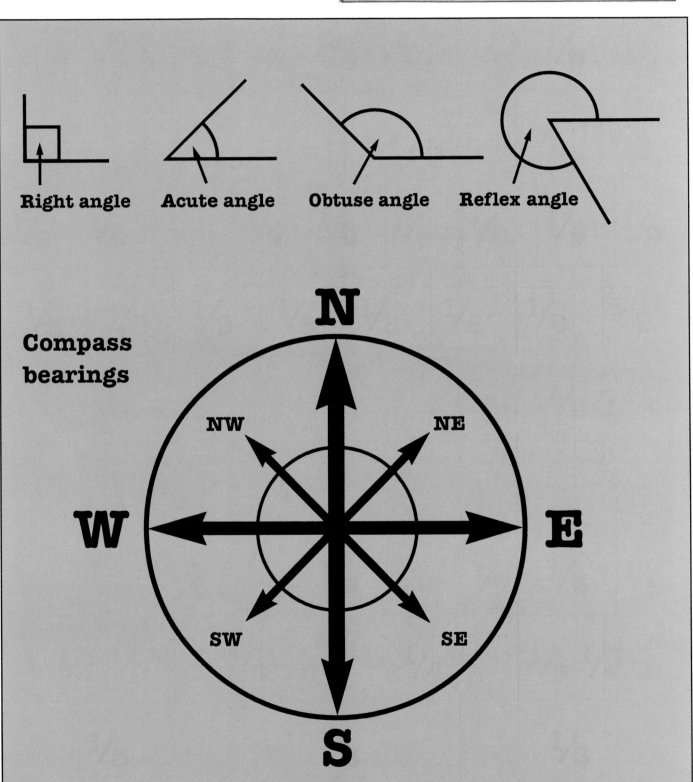

Right angle    Acute angle    Obtuse angle    Reflex angle

Compass bearings

**N**

NW    NE

**W**          **E**

SW    SE

**S**

# COMMON MEASUREMENTS

## AREA

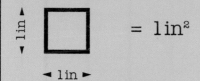

= 1in²

= 4in²

= 9in²

= 16in²

## LENGTH

12 inches = 1 foot

3 feet = 1 yard

1,760 yards = 1 mile

## VOLUME

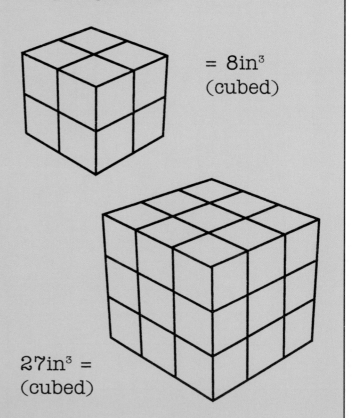

= 8in³
(cubed)

27in³ =
(cubed)

# TIME AND WEIGHT

## Time

60 seconds = 1 minute

60 minutes = 1 hour

24 hours = 1 day

## Weight

16 ounces = 1 pound

2000 pounds = 1 ton

## 24-hour clock

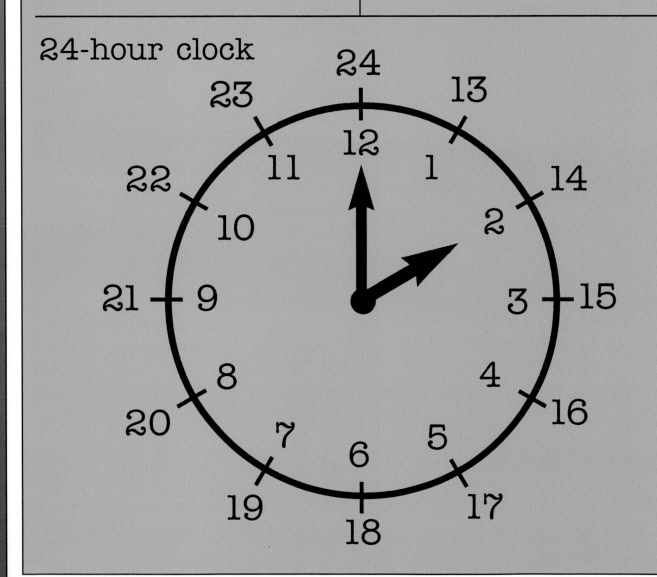

# GLOSSARY

**Addition**

When you use addition, two or more numbers are put together to find their total. The addition sign looks like this +, so 6+4=10.

**Algebra**

In problem solving, letters are sometimes used to represent numbers or other amounts such as height or weight. This is useful when there are no numbers to help you or you are not sure what the numbers or amounts might be. This kind of mathematics is called algebra.

**Angles**

Where two straight lines meet, they make an angle. We can measure these in degrees. An angle of 90 degrees is called a right angle.

**Area**

Area is the size of a space inside a flat shape. We can measure area by counting the number of squares that cover a shape.

**Arithmetic**

Arithmetic is the art of calculating with numbers. You use arithmetic when you solve number problems using addition, subtraction, multiplication, and division.

**Capacity**

Capacity is the way we measure the amount that something will hold. A jug that holds a pint of water has the capacity of one pint.

**Category**

If you were sorting animals into sets, first you would have to decide on the categories you wanted to use. One category could be animals that eat meat, so a lion and a dog would both belong to this category.

**Circle**

A circle is a round shape with one curved edge. The distance from the center of the circle to any point on its edge is always exactly the same.

**Circumference**

The circumference is the length all the way around the edge of a circle.

**Clockwise**

When you turn clockwise it means you turn in the same direction as the hands of a clock. If you turn counterclockwise, you turn in the opposite direction to the hands of a clock.

**Cone**

A cone is a solid shape. The base it stands on is a circle. Its curved surface goes up to a point at the top.

# GLOSSARY

**Coordinates**
Coordinates are two numbers that show where a point is in a space, for example, on a map or on a graph. The numbers (2,4) might show the position two places along and four places up a grid.

**Cubed inches**
A cubed inch is the volume of a cube measuring 1in long, 1in wide, and 1in high. One cubed inch is also written $1in^3$.

**Decimal**
We use a decimal number system. That means that we count in ones and groups of tens.

**Decimal point**
A decimal point separates the digits worth 1 or more on the left from digits less than 1 on the right. A decimal number looks like this 426.25.

**Degrees**
Angles can be measured in degrees. Mathematicians use the sign ° for degrees. A full turn is 360°. A quarter turn is 90°. A half turn is 180°. A three-quarter turn is 270°.

**Diameter**
The diameter is a line that cuts a circle exactly in half. It goes from the edge of the circle, through the center, and to the edge on the other side.

**Digit**
Numbers are made up of digits. There are two digits in the number 25: a 2 and a 5. There are three digits in the number 683: a 6, an 8, and a 3.

**Dimension**
We use dimensions to measure shapes. Flat shapes like circles or squares are 2D because they have two dimensions. We can measure how long and how wide they are. Solid shapes like cones and cubes are 3D because they have three dimensions. We can measure how long, how wide, and how high they are.

**Division**
Division is the opposite or inverse of multiplication. You could use division to find out how many 2s there are in 12. The division sign looks like this ÷ , so 12÷2=6.

**Element**
Each item that is in a set is called an element, so in a set of shoes, one shoe is an element of that set.

# GLOSSARY

**Equals**

The equals sign looks like this =. Whatever is on one side of the equals sign has to be the same amount as on the other side. Both sides must balance, so 7−1=3+1+2.

**Estimate**

An estimate is a careful guess. You could estimate how many petals you think there are on a daisy. When you have made an estimate, you could check it by counting the petals.

**Factor**

In multiplication, the numbers that you multiply together are the factors, so 6 and 2 are factors of 12.

**Fraction**

A fraction is part of a whole. A slice of pizza is a fraction of the whole pizza. A fraction looks like this: $^3/4$. The top number tells us how many parts of the whole there are in the fraction. The bottom number tells us how many parts the whole has been divided into.

**Function**

A function is a rule or a set of rules that are followed. A function could be "double the number and take 1 away," so the number 3 becomes 5 and the number 4 becomes 7.

**Graph**

A graph is a way of showing information so that it is quick and easy to understand and use. Pie charts, bar graphs, pictograms, and line graphs are all different types of graphs.

**Half**

A half is a fraction. We write it like this: $^1/2$. You get two halves when you divide something into two equal parts.

**Horizontal axis**

The horizontal axis is the line going across the bottom of a graph.

**Improper fraction**

Fractions bigger than a whole are called improper fractions. $^5/4$ is an improper fraction because the number on the top is larger than the number on the bottom.

**Inequality sign**

The inequality sign shows that one number is bigger or smaller than another. It looks like this < or like this >. Whatever is on the open side is larger, so 10>5.

# GLOSSARY

**Line of symmetry**
A line of symmetry cuts a shape in half so both halves look exactly the same.

**Mass**
Mass describes how much there is of something. Mass is sometimes used as another word for weight. It is often measured in ounces.

**Multiplication**
Multiplication is a way of adding the same number many times. The sign looks like this x. Six 2s can be written like this 2+2+2+2+2+2 or like this 6x2, so 6x2=12.

**Net**
A net is a flat shape made when the sides of a solid shape, like a cube, are opened out. When the net is folded and the sides are joined together it makes a solid shape again.

**Number patterns**
Number patterns are formed when something is repeated again and again. For example, a number pattern can be made when a group of numbers are repeated like this – 2, 3, 4, 2, 3, 4, 2, 3, 4. Doing something to a number, such as adding 3 again and again, makes another kind of number pattern like this – 1, 4, 7, 10.

**Percentage**
A percentage is a part of a hundred. A percent sign looks like this: %. 1% means 1 out of a hundred. 25% means 25 out of a hundred.

**Product**
The product is the number you get when you multiply other numbers together, so 12 is the product of 6x2.

**Property**
Items in a set all have properties or things that can describe them. One property of an apple is that it is a fruit. Another property is that it has a round shape. An apple can belong to a set of apples, or a set of things with a round shape, or to a set of fruit.

**Radius**
The radius is the distance from the center to the edge of a circle. Any straight line drawn from the center to the edge of a circle is called a radial line.

**Ratio**
A ratio is a way of comparing the amount of different things in a whole. If you mix two teaspoons of yellow paint to one teaspoon of red paint to make orange, you have used the ratio of 2:1 in your mixture.

# GLOSSARY

**Right angle**

A right angle is a quarter turn or 90°. The corners of squares and rectangles are all right angles.

**Rotational symmetry**

A shape has rotational symmetry if it looks exactly the same when it has been moved around a central point.

**Scale**

A scale is a machine we use for measuring how much things weigh. A kitchen scale measures light-weight things such as an apple, and a bathroom scale can measure heavy things like your mom and dad.

**Set**

When mathematicians put things into groups, each group is called a set. All the things in the set have something the same about them.

**Square inches**

A square inch is the area of a square with sides of one inch long. Four square inches can be written $4in^2$ and would fit into a square with sides of two inches long.

**Standard measurements**

The units of measurement we use, like inches, must always be the same or we cannot be sure how big anything is. Some standard units commonly used today are pints, fluid ounces, and feet.

**Subtraction**

Subtraction is the opposite of addition. When you subtract you take one number away from another to find their difference. The subtraction sign is sometimes known as minus and looks like this −, so $10 - 4 = 6$.

**Tenth**

If you divide something into ten equal parts, one of those parts is a tenth. A tenth can look like this: $1/10$. The number after a decimal point shows you tenths. So the digit 6, in the number 1.6, is 6 tenths.

**Vertical axis**

The vertical axis is the line going up the side of a graph.

**Volume**

The volume of a shape is the amount of space it takes up. You would take up much less space than an elephant. Volume is usually measured in cubic inches.

# INDEX

# INDEX